CONDEMNED
Without a Trial

CONDEMNED
Without a Trial

BOGUS ARGUMENTS AGAINST
BILINGUAL EDUCATION

STEPHEN D. KRASHEN

HEINEMANN
Portsmouth, NH

Heinemann
A division of Reed Elsevier Inc.
361 Hanover Street
Portsmouth, NH 03801–3912
http://www.heinemann.com

Offices and agents throughout the world

Library of Congress Cataloging-in-Publication Data
Krashen, Stephen D.
    Condemned without a trial : bogus arguments against bilingual
education / Stephen D. Krashen.
        p.   cm.
    Includes bibliographical references and index.
    ISBN 0-325-00129-4 (alk. paper)
    1. Education, Bilingual—United States.   2. Education, Bilingual—
United States—Public opinion.   3. United States—Public opinion.
4. Educational surveys—United States.   I. Title.
LC3731.K727   1999
370.117'5'0973—dc21   98-45356
                                                                    CIP

Editor: Lois Bridges
Production: Elizabeth Valway
Cover design: Catherine Hawkes, Cat and Mouse
Manufacturing: Louise Richardson

Printed in the United States of America on acid-free paper

03 02 01 00   DA   4 5

Contents

Introduction and Background

In the recent Proposition 227 campaign in California, a number of accusations were made about bilingual education: It was asserted that bilingual education was the cause of students dropping out of school, that school success was possible (and even more likely) without bilingual education because so many people had done well without it, that the United States was the only country that did bilingual education, and that public opinion was against it. It was also asserted that many districts had done better when they dropped their bilingual education programs.

In this monograph I argue that none of these accusations are true. These arguments follow from the framework developed in Krashen (1996), which I review briefly here, as well as some of the issues discussed in that volume.

Why Bilingual Education?

When schools provide children with quality education in their primary language, they give them two things: knowledge and literacy. The *knowledge* that children get through their first language helps make the English they hear and read more comprehensible. *Literacy* developed in the primary language transfers to the second language. The reason literacy transfers is simple: Because we learn to read by reading, by making sense of what is on the page (Smith

1994), it is easier to learn to read in a language we understand. Once we can read in one language, we can read in general.

Subject matter knowledge and literacy, gained through the primary language, provide indirect but powerful support for English language development and are two of the three components of quality bilingual programs. The third component, of course, is direct support for English language development, via English as a second language (ESL) classes and sheltered subject matter teaching, classes in which intermediate-level ESL students learn subject matter taught in English in a comprehensible way.

In gradual-exit bilingual programs, non-English-speaking children initially receive core subject matter instruction in the primary language, along with ESL instruction. As soon as possible, they receive sheltered subject matter instruction in those subjects that are the easiest to make comprehensible—in English, math, and science, which, at this level, do not demand a great deal of abstract use of language. In later stages, math and science are done in the mainstream and other subjects, such as social studies, are taught in sheltered classes in English. Eventually, all subjects are done in the mainstream. In this way, sheltered classes function as a bridge between instruction in the first language and the mainstream. Once full mainstreaming is complete, advanced first-language development is available as an option. This kind of plan avoids problems associated with exiting children too early from first-language instruction (before the English they encounter is comprehensible) and provides instruction in the first language where it is most needed. These plans also allow children to have the advantages of advanced first-language development.

Success Without Bilingual Education?

A common argument against bilingual education is the observation that many people have succeeded without it. This has cer-

	MAINSTREAM	ESL/SHELTERED	FIRST LANGUAGE
Beginning	Art, music, PE	ESL	All core subjects
Intermediate	Art, music, PE	ESL, math, science	Social studies, language arts
Advanced	Art, music, PE Math, science	ESL, social studies	Language arts
Mainstream	All subjects		Heritage language development

tainly happened. In these cases, however, the successful person got plenty of comprehensible input in the second language, and in many cases had a de facto bilingual education program. Examples are Rodriguez and de la Pena.

Rodriguez (1982) tells us that he succeeded in school without a special program and acquired a very high level of English literacy. He had two crucial advantages, however, that most limited English proficient (LEP) children do not have. First, he grew up in an English-speaking neighborhood in Sacramento, California, and thus got a great deal of comprehensible input from classmates. Many limited English proficient children encounter English only at school; they live in neighborhoods where the first language prevails. In addition, Rodriguez became a voracious reader, which helped him acquire academic language. Most LEP children have little access to books.

De la Pena (1991) reports that he came to the United States at age nine with no English competence and claims that he succeeded without bilingual education. He reports that he acquired English rapidly, and, "by the end of my first school year, I was among the top students." De la Pena, however, had the advantages of bilingual education: In Mexico, he was in the fifth grade, and was thus literate in Spanish and knew subject matter. In addition, when he started school in the United States he was put back two grades. His superior knowledge of the subject matter helped make the English he heard comprehensible. There are many additional cases similar to this one (Krashen 1996; Ramos and Krashen 1997), as well as studies (Krashen 1997) that confirm that children who arrive with a good education in their primary language do well. These children have already gained two of three objectives of a good bilingual education program—literacy and subject matter knowledge. Their success is strong evidence for bilingual education.

What About Languages Other Than Spanish?

Porter (1990) states, "even if there were a demonstrable advantage for Spanish-speakers learning to read first in their home language, it does not follow that the same holds true for speakers of language that do not use the Roman alphabet" (65). But it does. The ability to read transfers across languages, even when the writing systems are different. Studies cited in Krashen (1996) confirm that reading ability transfers from Chinese to English, Vietnamese to English, Japanese to English, and Turkish to Dutch, and there is also evidence that literacy transfers from Arabic to French (Wagner, Spratt, and Ezzaki 1989).

Bilingual Education and Public Opinion

Opponents of bilingual education tell us that the public is against bilingual education. This impression is a result of the way the question is asked. One can easily get a near 100 percent rejection of bilingual education when the question is biased. Quite often, the question asked presupposes that education in the first language is bad for English or that bilingual education delays English. Consider this question, asked by the Center for Equal Opportunity (1996):

> In your opinion, should children of Hispanic background, living in the United States, be taught to read and write Spanish before they are taught English, or should they be taught English as soon as possible?

One would expect parents to respond that children should be taught English as soon as possible. The way the question is phrased, however, suggests that learning to read and write in the first language will delay the acquisition of English. But bilingual education can contribute to the rapid acquisition of English.

A series of studies by Shin and colleagues (Shin and Gribbons 1996; Shin and Lee 1996; Shin and Kim 1996) shows that when bilingual education is carefully defined, support is high. Shin found that many interviewees agreed that developing literacy in the first language helped literacy development in English, that subject matter learning in the primary language was useful in making subject matter in English more comprehensible, and that continuing first-language development had cognitive and economic benefits.

The number of people opposed to bilingual education is probably even less than these results suggest. Many people who say they are opposed to bilingual education are actually opposed to certain practices (e.g., inappropriate placement of children) or are opposed to regulations connected to bilingual education (e.g., forcing teachers to acquire another language to keep their jobs).

Despite what is presented to the public in the media, there is support for bilingual education. McQuillan and Tse (1996) reviewed publications appearing between 1984 and 1994, and reported that 87 percent of academic publications supported bilingual education, but newspaper and magazine articles tended to be anti–bilingual education, with only 45 percent supporting bilingual education. In addition, less than half of the opinion articles about bilingual education referred to educational research. One wonders what public support would look like if bilingual education were covered more accurately in the press.

The Research Debate

It is sometimes claimed that research does not support the efficacy of bilingual education. Its harshest critics, however (e.g., Rossell and Baker 1996), do not claim that bilingual education does not work; instead, they claim there is little evidence that it is superior to all-English programs. The evidence used against bilingual education is not convincing. One major problem is labeling. Several critics, for example, have claimed that "English immersion" programs in El Paso and McAllen, Texas, were superior to bilingual education. In each case, however, programs labeled "immersion" were really bilingual education, with a substantial part of the day taught in the primary language. In another study, Gersten (1985) claimed that all-English immersion was better than bilingual education. However, the sample size was very small and the duration of the study was short; also, no description of "bilingual education" was provided. For a detailed discussion of these issues, see Krashen (1996).

On the other hand, a vast number of studies have shown that bilingual education *is* effective, with children in well-designed bilingual programs acquiring academic English as well as, and often better than, children in all-English programs (Willig 1985; Cummins 1989; Krashen 1996). Willig concluded that the better the experimental design, the more positive were the effects of bilingual education.

Improving Bilingual Education

Bilingual education has done well, but it can do much better. The biggest problem, in my view, is the absence of books, in both the first and second language, in the lives of students in these programs. Free voluntary reading can help all components of bilingual education: It is a source of comprehensible input in English, a means for developing knowledge and literacy in the first language, and a way of continuing first-language development.

Limited English proficient Spanish-speaking children have little access to books at home (about twenty-two books per home for the entire family according to Ramirez et al. 1991) or at school (an average of one book in Spanish per Spanish-speaking child in some school libraries in schools with bilingual programs, according to Pucci 1994). A book flood in both languages is clearly called for. Good bilingual programs have brought students to the 50th percentile on standardized tests of English reading by grade 5 (Burnham-Massey and Pena 1990). But with a good supply of books, students can go far beyond the 50th percentile. We may even get the Lake Wobegon effect, where all of the children are above average. We can finally do away with the tests, and put the money saved to much better use.

This Volume

The arguments I present here are easy to summarize:

- Chapter 1 argues that bilingual education is not the cause of dropping out of school; it may be the cure for dropping out. Studies show reduced and even no differences among groups in dropout rates when background variables, such as poverty, are considered. (Earlier versions of this chapter were published in the *CABE Newsletter*, 1998, 21 [4], and by the National Bilingual Education Clearinghouse.)

- Chapter 2 presents more evidence for the value of education in the primary language. I argued in Krashen (1996) and above that many of those who did well without bilingual education had de facto bilingual education, that is, subject matter and literacy development in their own language before they came to the United States. I present more data here that this is the case. In addition, I discuss economic success without bilingual education: Several scholars have argued that immigrants did not do very well in school in the first part of the twentieth century; economic success, however, was not dependent on school success. (Originally published in the *CABE Newsletter*, 1997, 21 [2]: 8, 23.)

- Chapter 3 surveys bilingual programs of various kinds outside the United States, answering critics who argue that other countries do not do bilingual education, and therefore it should not be done in the United States. Not only is bilingual education widespread but also, wherever it has been evaluated abroad the results have been quite positive. (An earlier version of this chapter was published in the *CABE Newsletter*, 1998, 21 [5]:14, 35–36.)

- Chapter 4 reviews cases in which it was announced that all-English alternatives were superior to bilingual education. In no case was this true.

- Chapter 5 continues the discussion of public opinion polls begun in Krashen (1996). It focuses on differences of interpretation of polls between Rossell and Baker (1996) and Krashen (1996), and concludes once again that public opinion is not anti–bilingual education. In a postscript to this chapter, I argue that this was also the case during the Proposition 227 debate in California. Although the public voted to eliminate bilingual education, polls indicated support for use of the first language in school, a strange result that suggests that a substantial number of voters who supported 227 were not aware of what was in it. (An earlier version of this chapter was published in the *Bilingual Research Journal*, 1996, 20: 411–431.)

• The final chapter reviews an important recent study by Jay Greene. Greene utilized "meta-analysis," a method of summarizing a group of studies in a precise way. It takes into consideration not only if one group did better than another, but also just how much better they did (see also Willig 1985). Greene reported that limited English proficient children who were in bilingual programs significantly outperformed those in comparison groups. The difference was modest, but I argue that Greene may have underestimated the effect of bilingual education. This paper makes an important contribution to the continuing debate over the effectiveness of bilingual education.

References

Burnham-Massey, L., and M. Pena. 1990. "Effects of Bilingual Instruction on English Academic Achievement of LEP students." *Reading Improvement* 27 (2): 129–132.

Center for Equal Opportunity. 1996. *The Importance of Learning English.* Washington, DC: Center for Equal Opportunity.

Cummins, J. 1989. *Empowering Minority Students.* Ontario, CA: California Association for Bilingual Education.

de la Pena, F. 1991. *Democracy or Babel? The Case for Official English in the United States.* Washington, DC: U.S. English.

Gersten, R. 1985. "Structured Immersion for Language-Minority Students: Results of a Longitudinal Evaluation." *Educational Evaluation and Policy Analysis* 7 (3): 187–196.

Krashen, S. 1996. *Under Attack: The Case Against Bilingual Education.* Culver City, CA: Language Education Associates.

———. 1997. "(Still More) Evidence for the Value of Education in the Primary Language (de facto Bilingual Education)." *CABE Newsletter* 21 (2): 8, 23.

McQuillan, J., and L. Tse. 1996. "Does Research Really Matter? An Analysis of Media Opinion on Bilingual Education, 1984–1994." *Bilingual Research Journal* 20 (1): 1–27.

Porter, R. 1990. *Forked Tongue: The Politics of Bilingual Education.* New York: Basic Books.

Pucci, S. 1994. "Supporting Spanish Language Literacy: Latino Children and Free Reading Resources in Schools." *Bilingual Research Journal* 18 (1–2): 67–82.

Ramirez, J., D. Yuen, D. Ramey, and D. Pasta. 1991. *Longitudinal Study of Structured English Immersion Strategy, Early-Exit and Late-Exit Bilingual Education Programs for Language-Minority Students.* Final report, vols. 1 and 2. San Mateo, CA: Aguirre International. ERIC Document ED 330 216.

Ramos, F., and S. Krashen. 1997. "Success Without Bilingual Education? Some European Cases of de facto Bilingual Education." *CABE Newsletter* 20 (6): 7, 19.

Rodriquez, R. 1982. *Hunger of Memory: The Education of Richard Rodriquez.* New York: Bantam Books.

Rossell, C., and K. Baker. 1996. "The Educational Effectiveness of Bilingual Education." *Research in the Teaching of English* 30 (1): 7–74.

Shin, F. 1994. "Attitudes of Korean Parents Toward Bilingual Education." *BE Outreach Newsletter.* California State Department of Education 5 (2): 47–48.

Shin, F., and B. Gribbons. 1996. "Hispanic Parents' Perceptions and Attitudes of Bilingual Education." *Journal of Mexican-American Educators* 16–22.

Shin, F., and S. Kim. 1996. "Korean Parent Perceptions and Attitudes of Bilingual Education." In *Current Issues in Asian and Pacific American Education*, edited by R. Endo, C. Park, J. Tsuchida, and A. Abbayani. Covina, CA: Pacific Asian Press.

Shin, F., and B. Lee. 1996. "Hmong Parents: What Do They Think About Bilingual Education?" *Pacific Educational Research Journal* 8: 65–71.

Smith, F. 1994. *Understanding Reading.* 5th ed. Hillsdale, NJ: Erlbaum.

Wagner, D., J. Spratt, and A. Ezzaki. 1989. "Does Learning to Read in a Second Language Always Put the Child at a Disadvantage? Some Counter-Evidence from Morocco." *Applied Psycholinguistics* 10: 31–48.

Willig, A. 1985. "A Meta-Analysis of Selected Studies on the Effectiveness of Bilingual Education." *Review of Educational Research* 55 (3): 269–317.

1

Bogus Argument #1

Bilingual Education Is Responsible for the High Hispanic Dropout Rate

Critics of bilingual education have cited the high Hispanic dropout rate as evidence against bilingual education. Since most bilingual programs are Spanish-English, it is concluded that bilingual education must be responsible. In this chapter, I review what is known about dropout rates among Hispanic students and refute the notion that bilingual education causes students to drop out.

Do Hispanic Students Drop Out More?

The latest figures from the U.S. government on school dropout rates have been recently released, covering the academic year 1994–1995 (McMillen, Kaufman, and Klein 1997). Defining the dropout rate as the proportion of young adults (ages 16 to 24) who are not enrolled in a high school program and who have not completed high school, there is no question that Hispanic students have higher dropout rates: 30 percent of Hispanic young adults were classified as dropouts, compared to 8.6 percent for non-Hispanic whites and 12.1 percent for non-Hispanic blacks.

Among Hispanic young adults, however, dropout figures include many who never enrolled in school, such as foreign-born immigrants who apparently came to the United States for work and not education (31). The government report calculates that about one-third of the 30 percent dropout figure for Hispanic young adults is due to non-enrollees. The true Hispanic dropout rate is thus about 20 percent.

Is Bilingual Education to Blame?

It is true that most students in bilingual education speak Spanish, but not all Spanish-speaking children are in bilingual education. Far from it. Fewer than half of the Spanish-speaking children in school in California are limited English proficient (Han, Baker, and Rodriguez 1997; Snyder and Hoffman 1996). Of these, not all are in programs that provide instruction in the primary language; according to Macias (1997), about 30 percent of limited English proficient children were in programs that had academic instruction in the primary language while another 22 percent had "informal" support in the first language. Thus, most Spanish-speaking children are *not* in bilingual education.[1] Since the 20 percent dropout figure applies to all Spanish-speaking children, we can assume that most of those who dropped out were not in bilingual education.

Some Direct Evidence

There is evidence showing that bilingual education is not only blameless, but actually results in lower dropout rates. Curiel, Rosenthal, and Richek (1986) compared dropout rates for eighty-six students who had had one or more years of bilingual education with a similar group ($N = 90$) who had not had bilingual education. Considering all dropouts between grades 7 and 11, Curiel, Rosenthal, and Richek reported that those who had had bilingual education were significantly less likely to drop out (23.5 percent versus 43 percent). Most of this difference was due to those who dropped out before high school (8.1 percent versus 25.8 percent).

What Accounts for Dropout Rates?

If bilingual education is not the problem, what is? Not surprisingly, English language speaking ability is a factor. Limiting the analysis to those who actually enrolled in school, those who reported speaking English "not well" had a 32.9 percent dropout rate, while those who spoke English well or very well had a 19.2 percent dropout rate (McMillen, Kaufman, and Klein 1997). This is not an argument against bilingual education, because studies have shown that children in well-designed bilingual programs do well in English (Willig 1985; Krashen 1996; Greene 1998).

Several "background factors" have been identified as consistent predictors of dropping out: Socioeconomic class, time spent in the United States, the presence of print, and family factors. Students in wealthier families drop out less, those who have been here longer and who live in a more print-rich environment drop out less, those who live with both parents and whose parents monitor schoolwork drop out less, and those who do not become teen parents drop out less.

Hispanic students are well behind majority children in these areas. Approximately 40 percent of Hispanic children live in poverty, compared to 15 percent of white non-Hispanic children, and 45 percent live with parents who have completed high school, compared to 81 percent of non-Hispanic white children. Only 68 percent live with both parents, compared to 81 percent of non-Hispanic white children (Rumberger 1991).

What is of great interest to us is that *these background factors appear to be responsible for much if not all of the difference in dropout rates among different ethnic groups.* In other words, when researchers control for these factors, there is little or no difference in dropout rates between Hispanics and other groups. This result holds for those who drop out between grades 8 and 10 (Rumberger 1995) as well as for those who drop out later (Rumberger 1983; Fernandez, Paulsen, and Hiranko-Nakanishi 1989; Warren 1996; White and Kaufman 1997; Pirog and Magee 1997).

Rumberger (1995), for example, concluded: "Black, Hispanic, and Native American students have twice the odds of dropping out compared to White students . . . however, after controlling for the structural characteristics of family background—particularly, socioeconomic status—the predicted odds of dropping out are no different than those for White students" (605).

White and Kaufman (1997), in their study of high school dropouts between 1980 and 1986, provide a clear example of the impact of these factors. See table on page 5. Note that new immigrants from Mexico without economic and family factors working in their favor have a higher probability of dropping out than those from other groups. Mexican students with high socioeconomic status (SES) and high social capital, however, show no significant difference in the probability of dropping out compared to other groups.

Additional evidence that there is strong economic pressure on many Hispanic students comes from Rumberger (1983). When asked to list their reasons for dropping out, only 4 percent of Hispanic male dropouts said that the reason was "poor performance" in school (compared to 8 percent of male non-Hispanic white students). Thirty-eight percent of the Hispanic students gave economic reasons (desire to work, financial difficulties, home responsibilities), compared to 22 percent of the non-Hispanic white students. Similar tendencies were present for female dropouts.

PROBABILITIES OF DROPPING OUT OF HIGH SCHOOL: IMPACT OF SES, SOCIAL CAPITAL,ᵃ GENERATION

White—low SES, low social capital = .23

Black—low SES, low social capital = .22

White—high SES, high social capital = .08

Black—high SES, high social capital = .08

Mexican—immigrant, less than 6 years in U.S., low SES, low social capital = .40

Mexican—immigrant, more than 6 years, high SES, high social capital = .12

Mexican—second generation or native, high SES, high social capital = .10

Asian—immigrant, less than 6 years in U.S., low SES, low social capital = .31

Asian—immigrant, more than 6 years in U.S., high SES, high social capital = .08

Asian—second generation or native, high SES, high social capital = .07

ᵃsocial capital = living with both parents, parents monitor schoolwork, siblings in college

Source: White and Kaufman (1997)

In some studies, the dropout differences between Hispanics and other groups remain after background factors are controlled, but the differences are reduced enormously. Warren (1996) reported that Mexican immigrant students were 24 percent as likely to make it to grade 12 as non-Hispanic white students, but when factors such as the education and occupation of the head of the household and the size of the family were controlled, this group was 71 percent as likely to reach grade 12. (See also Fernandez, Paulsen, and Hiranko-Nakanishi 1989.)

Does Spanish Language Development Increase the Odds of Dropping Out?

The U.S. Government report (McMillen, Kaufman, and Klein 1997) found that for those Hispanic young adults who were enrolled in school in the United States, there is no difference in dropout rates between those who said they spoke Spanish at home (20.3 percent) and those who said they spoke English at home (17.5 percent). White and Kaufman (1997) and Rumberger (1995) report similar results. One study reported that those who rated themselves higher in Spanish dropped out more (Fernandez, Paulsen, and Hiranko-Nakanishi 1989), but the effect was not large. For each unit change in self-assessed Spanish proficiency, on a scale of 0 (lowest) to 4 (highest), the chances of dropping out increased only 3.4 percent.

Rumbaut (1995) examined the progress of over 15,000 high school students in San Diego who were children of foreign-born parents. Predictably, those classified as limited English proficient had lower grade-point averages and were more likely to drop out. What is very interesting, however, is that those classified as "fluent English proficient" (in other words, former limited English proficient students who were now bilingual), had better grades and slightly lower dropout rates than those rated English-only. This was the case even though parents of English-only students were of higher socioeconomic status than parents of the bilingual students.

There is thus no firm evidence that Spanish language development leads to dropping out, and some evidence that suggests that maintenance of the Spanish language and culture may prevent it.

Conclusions

Some factors predicting dropout rates have been identified: low English language ability, poverty, length of residence in the United States, the print environment, and family factors. The important finding from the research is that when these factors are controlled statistically, the dropout rate among Hispanics is the same or nearly the same as that of other groups. There is no "Hispanic dropout mystery" (Headden 1997).

There is no evidence that bilingual education results in higher dropout rates. A minority of Hispanic children in California are in bilingual programs, and the reported dropout rates refer to all Hispanic children. In fact, because well-designed bilingual programs produce better academic English (Krashen 1996), bilingual education is part of the cure, not the disease, as Curiel, Rosenthal, and Richek's study shows. Good bilingual programs have this effect because they supply subject matter knowledge in the students' primary language, which makes the English the students hear and read much more comprehensible. They also provide a rapid route to literacy: It is much easier to learn to read in a language one already understands, and once literacy is developed, it transfers rapidly to the second language.

Another part of the cure is simple and inexpensive: an improved print environment in school. As noted earlier, the presence of print is a predictor of dropping out, as is low socioeconomic status. It is also well established that children of poverty typically live in environments with few books (see, Smith, Constantino, and Krashen 1997; McQuillan 1998). In addition, we know that the amount of free voluntary reading done is an excellent predictor of literacy development and that children read more when they have more access to books and are read to more (Krashen 1993; McQuillan 1998). Improving the print environment in both the primary language and in

English—through better school libraries and classroom libraries and by encouraging free reading in both languages through read-alouds (Trelease 1995), sustained silent reading (Krashen 1993), and quality literature programs—promises to increase literacy development in both languages, which will make a powerful contribution to school success.

Note

1. California data tells us how many LEP children are in bilingual programs but does not break this down by native language. Jim Crawford has pointed out to me, however, that 96.3 percent of bilingual teachers provide instruction in Spanish. We can thus assume that about 96 percent of the children are in Spanish language programs. If so, 36 percent of Spanish language LEP children were in full bilingual programs in California in 1997 (total Spanish-speaking LEP = 1,107,186; total in bilingual education = 410,127; estimate of Spanish-speaking LEP in bilingual education = 394,952).

References

Curiel, H., J. Rosenthal, and H. Richek. 1986. "Impacts of Bilingual Education on Secondary School Grades, Attendance, Retentions and Dropouts." *Hispanic Journal of Behavioral Sciences* 8 (4): 357–367.

Fernandez, R., R. Paulsen, and M. Hiranko-Nakanishi. 1989. "Dropping Out Among Hispanic Youth." *Social Science Research* 18: 21–52.

Greene, J. 1998. *A Meta-Analysis of the Effectiveness of Bilingual Education.* Claremont, CA: Tomas Rivera Policy Institute.

Han, M., D. Baker, and C. Rodriguez. 1997. *A Profile of Policies and Practices for Limited English Proficient Students: Screening Methods, Program Support, and Teacher Training.* Washington, DC: U.S. Department of Education, NCES 97–472.

Headden, S. 1997. "The Hispanic Dropout Mystery." *US News and World Report* (October 20): 64–65.

Krashen, S. 1993. *The Power of Reading*. Englewood, CO: Libraries Unlimited.

———. 1996. *Under Attack: The Case Against Bilingual Education*. Culver City, CA: Language Education Associates.

Macias, R. 1997. "CA LEP Enrollment Slows but Continues to Rise." *LMRI (Linguistic Minority Research Institute)* 7 (1): 1–2.

McMillen, M., P. Kaufman, and S. Klein. 1997. *Dropout Rates in the United States: 1995*. Washington, DC: U.S. Department of Education. NCES 97–473.

McQuillan, J. 1998. *The Literacy Crisis: False Claims and Real Solutions*. Portsmouth, NH: Heinemann.

Pirog, M., and C. Magee. 1997. "High School Completion: The Influence of Schools, Families, and Adolescent Parenting." *Social Science Quarterly* 78: 710–724.

Rumbaut, R. 1995. "The New Californians: Comparative Research Findings on the Educational Progress of Immigrant Children." In *California's Immigrant Children*, edited by R. Rumbaut and W. Cornelius. University of California, San Diego: Center for U.S.-Mexican Studies. 17–69.

Rumberger, R. 1983. "Dropping Out of High School: The Influence of Race, Sex, and Family Background." *American Educational Research Journal* 20 (2): 199–220.

———. 1991. "Chicano Dropouts: A Review of Research and Policy Issues." In *Chicano School Failure and Success*, edited by R. Valencia. New York: Falmer Press.

———. 1995. "Dropping Out of Middle School: A Multilevel Analysis of Students and Schools." *American Educational Research Journal* 32 (3): 583–625.

Smith, C., R. Constantino, and S. Krashen. 1997. "Differences in Print Environment for Children in Beverly Hills, Compton, and Watts." *Emergency Librarian* 24 (4): 4–5.

Snyder, T., and D. Hoffman. 1996. *Digest of Educational Statistics*. Washington, DC: National Center for Educational Statistics, U.S. Department of Education.

Trelease, J. 1995. *The Read-Aloud Handbook*. New York: Penguin.

Warren, J. 1996. "Educational Inequality Among White and Mexican-Origin Adolescents in the American Southwest." *Sociology of Education* 69: 142–158.

White, M., and G. Kaufman. 1997. "Language Usage, Social Capital, and School Completion Among Immigrants and Native-Born Ethnic Groups." *Social Science Quarterly* 78 (2): 385–398.

Willig, A. 1985. "A Meta-Analysis of Selected Studies on the Effectiveness of Bilingual Education." *Review of Educational Research* 55 (3): 269–317.

2

Bogus Argument #2

Most Immigrants Succeeded Without Bilingual Education (or, still more evidence for the value of eduation in the primary language)

I t has been suggested that the value of education in the first language is due to two related contributions: Subject matter knowledge gained in the first language makes English input more comprehensible, and literacy developed in the first language facilitates literacy development in English. Good bilingual programs attempt to provide these two components.

This analysis helps to explain cases of "success without bilingual education." Those who do well in English academic language development have frequently had a good education in their primary language before coming to the United States (Krashen 1996). The universality of this phenomenon was confirmed by Ramos and Krashen (1997), who reported success stories of educated immigrants to Spain and by Tse (1997), who not only was educated in her first language when she arrived in the United States, but also had help in schoolwork in the first language after she arrived from family members.

I present here additional cases that confirm the existence of this phenomenon and that show its great strength, as well as its robustness: It is found using different research techniques and among different groups.

Gardner, Polyzoi, and Rampaul (1996) studied the impact of education in the first language on progress in intensive ESL classes for Kurdish and Bosnian adult immigrants to Canada who had "virtually no English" when they arrived (1996, 3). The subjects were classified into three groups, as presented in Table 2–1.

Table 2–2 presents the gains made by each group on tests of oral and written English after participation in intensive ESL (twenty hours per week, for one to one and a half years). For both measures, it is clear that the higher the level of literacy in the primary language, the greater the gains. This was true of both measures, and extremely powerful in the written test, in which preliterates' posttest scores were lower than the high literates' pretest scores.

Three independent studies using multiple regression arrive at conclusions similar to those of Gardner, Polyzoi, and Rampaul.

Table 2–1
Characteristics of Subjects

SUBJECTS	N	YEARS OF FORMAL EDUCATION	AGE[a]	LENGTH OF STUDY[b]
High literates	6	15	31	18
Semiliterates	4	7	28	21
Preliterates	4	0	35	21

[a] age of arrival in Canada
[b] months in ESL program

Source: Gardner, Polyzoi, and Rampaul (1996)

Table 2–2
Gains After Intensive ESL Instruction

ORAL TEST SCORES[a]	PRE	POST
High literates	10	71
Semiliterates	7	58
Preliterates	1	43
WRITTEN TEST SCORES[b]	**PRE**	**POST**
High literates	17	91
Semiliterates	0	48
Preliterates	1	10

perfect score = 100 for both tests

[a]oral test: personal questions, picture description, discussion of leisure activities, family
[b]written test: write name, circle correct time, copy words, label pictures, answer personal questions, read text and write answers to questions, fill in blanks with correct prepositions, verb tenses, multiple choice vocabulary

Source: Gardner, Polyzoi, and Rampaul (1996)

Chiswick (1991) studied the determinants of English language proficiency in 836 illegal aliens who had been apprehended in Los Angeles in 1986–1987. Chiswick reported a positive relationship between years of education in the home country and English proficiency, with each year of additional schooling raising English fluency and reading ability 1.3 percent.

Chiswick and Miller (1995) studied 4,166 immigrants to Australia, based on the 1981 and 1986 censuses. For those who immigrated to Australia from non-English speaking countries, each year of education in the home country raised English fluency 3.6 percent in the 1981 sample and 3.3 percent in the 1986 sample.

Espenshade and Fu (1997) studied predictors of English competence among 4,146 immigrants to the United States (November 1989 Current Population Survey). Again, years of education in the home country before immigration was a significant predictor of English language proficiency.

All three studies controlled for the length of time the immigrant had been in the country and age at the time of immigration, and all considered the country of origin. But there were differences: Espenshade and Fu and Chiswick and Miller controlled for aspects of family and community life, and Chiswick included competence in English on arrival in the United States.

The samples were different: Subjects in Chiswick (1991) and Chiswick and Miller (1995) were men, but differed in mean age (23 versus 42.1 years), amount of education in the home country (7.1 versus 10.7 years), and duration of stay in the host country (1.5 versus 19.8 years). Espenshade and Fu's subjects included men and women but gender was controlled statistically.

All three studies relied on self-report of English, with subjects responding on a four-point scale: not at all, not well, well, and very well. Different interpretations, however, were used. Espenshade and Fu simply used a four-point scale, with 0 corresponding to "not at all" and 3 corresponding to "very well." Chiswick assigned a score of 0 for "not well" and "not at all" and 1 for "very well" and "well" but Chiswick and Miller assigned 0 to everything except "very well."

Despite there differences, the results of the three multiple regression studies are very similar, attesting to the robustness of the phenomenon. (Chiswick and Miller also cite other studies done with immigrants to Israel and Canada in which education in the home country was a significant predictor of proficiency in the language of the country.)

The positive effect of education in the primary language is accepted without comment or controversy in these studies. In fact, the multiple regression studies discussed here did not have the role of education in the primary language as their major focus. What is interesting is that the idea of supplying such education after immigration, as we do in bilingual education, is not mentioned as a possibility in any of the studies discussed here. One wonders how the low literates in Gardner, Polyzoi, and Rampaul, for example, would have progressed if they had been given the opportunity of developing first-language literacy and learning some subject matter in their first language after immigration.[1]

Note

1. None of the studies considered the amount of EFL (English as a foreign language) study subjects had. It could thus be argued that more education in the home country simply meant more EFL, and that EFL was the cause of better English proficiency. Recall that in Gardner, Polyzoi, and Rampaul, subjects arrived with "virtually no English," thus controlling for this variable. Also, in Espenshade and Fu (1997), English proficiency at arrival was controlled, which in effect controls for EFL study.

None of the regression studies included the impact of ESL in the host country. If those with more home country education are more likely to enroll in ESL, this is an alternative explanation for their higher proficiency in English. Note that Gardner, Polyzoi, and Rampaul show that those with more home country education profit more from ESL. Thus, even if those with more home language education do more ESL in the host country, education in the home country, in the primary language, is still advantageous.

References

Chiswick, B. 1991. "Speaking, Reading, and Earnings Among Low-Skilled Immigrants." *Journal of Labor Economics* 9: 149–170.

Chiswick, B., and P. Miller. 1995. "The Endogeneity Between Language and Earnings: International Analyses." *Journal of Labor Economics* 13: 246–288.

Espenshade, T., and H. Fu. 1997. "An Analysis of English-Language Proficiency Among U.S. Immigrants." *American Sociological Review* 62: 288–305.

Gardner, S., E. Polyzoi, and Y. Rampaul. 1996. "Individual Variables, Literacy History, and ESL Progress Among Kurdish and Bosnian Immigrants." *TESL Canada* 14: 1–20.

Krashen, S. 1996. *Under Attack: The Case Against Bilingual Education.* Culver City, CA: Language Education Associates.

Ramos, F., and S. Krashen. 1997. "Success Without Bilingual Education? Some European Cases of de facto Bilingual Education." *CABE Newsletter* 20 (6): 7, 19.

Tse, L. 1997. "A Bilingual Helping Hand." *Los Angeles Times,* 17 December.

Epilogue: Economic Success Without Bilingual Education?

The studies discussed in this section focus only on one aspect of immigrant success, the acquisition of academic English. What about economic success? It is frequently argued that many immigrants who arrived in the United States in the first part of the twentieth century did well economically without bilingual education. It is well established, however, that immigrants did not do all that well in school during this time, and that economic success in the first part of the twentieth century did not require school success.

I first point out, as others have (Parker 1986; Rothstein

1998), that immigrants did not typically succeed in school in the good old days. Data presented in the table below, from Olneck and Lazerson (1974) is typical: The dropout rate in Cleveland in 1908 among students with home languages other than English was far higher than the dropout rate among those who spoke English at home: Only 2 percent of Polish and Italian speakers reached high school, compared to 14 percent of English-speaking children. There was little improvement of the situation in 1916:

PERCENTAGE OF STUDENTS WHO REACHED HIGH SCHOOL IN CLEVELAND		
Home language	1908 (%)	1916 (%)
English	14	17
German	7	14
Yiddish	5	9
Italian	2	2
Polish	2	3

Source: Olneck and Lazerson 1974, 461, Table 7.

Clearly the dropout rate for all students was much much higher than what we see today, but among those who spoke a language other than English at home it was at least 90 percent.

It is not at all clear whether immigrants did better in school then they are doing today, relative to nonimmigrants. Direct comparisons are difficult, because of different definitions of dropping out and the powerful influence of nonschool factors in predicting dropout rates (e.g., Rumberger 1983, 1991, 1995). But a crude comparison is possible. To get an estimate of dropout rates today, I will use the "cohort" definition from McMillen and Kaufman (1997), the percent of eighth graders in 1988 who did not complete high school by 1994. For white non-Hispanics, the dropout rate was 5.7 percent. For Hispanic students, it was 14.3 percent. Thus, Hispanic students drop out at 2.5 times the rate as non-Hispanic whites at the present time.

In 1908, it was reported that 22 percent of students whose fathers were born in the United States and who entered high school in New York, Chicago, and Boston, reached their senior year while only 8 percent of students whose fathers were born in Italy did. In a study in 1922 in Connecticut, findings were similar, with 44 percent of those with U.S.-born fathers reaching the senior year while only 17 percent of those whose fathers were Italian-born (Olneck and Lazerson 1974) did so. Rothstein (1998) notes that in 1931, only 11 percent of the Italian students who entered high school graduated, compared to an overall rate of 40 percent. Italian immigrants dropped out at 2.75 times the rate of nonimmigrant students in the first study, at 2.6 times the rate in the second study, and 3.6 times the rate in the third. In the modern estimate, the data is flawed by the fact that only about 50 percent of Hispanic students are limited English proficient, and we have no data on how many of the Italian students were limited in English. Nor are other important factors considered. But what we can conclude is that immigrant students were not dramatically more successful in school in the first half of the twentieth century, either in absolute standards or when compared to others.

Rothstein (1998) provides additional evidence for this assertion, noting that participation in high school compared to the total school population for Jewish students in 1910 was considerably lower than that seen for Hispanic students today. I summarize his argument in the following table:

	TOTAL NUMBER IN SCHOOL	TOTAL NUMBER IN HS	PERCENTAGE OF TOTAL IN HS
Jewish, N.Y., 1910	191,000	6,000	3
Hispanic, L.A., 1996	390,000	103,000	26

Again, a lot is missing, but it is hard to conclude that immigrants were more successful then than they are now.

If immigrants did so poorly in school, how did they succeed? In the first part of the twentieth century, education was not a prerequisite to economic success. It is now. Years ago, there was work in manufacturing and agriculture that did not require high school or college. Today, nearly all work that leads to a decent living requires education.

The U.S. government defines the poverty level as earning about $7,800 or lower for a single person and about $15,500 or less for a family of four (U.S. Bureau of the Census: 1997, Table 738). Income levels are closely correlated with education (U.S. Bureau of the Census: 1997, Table 246) and those who are not high school graduates earn under the poverty ceiling if they are the sole provider for a family of four:

	EARNINGS ($)
Not a HS grad	14,000
HS grad	21,400
College grad	37,000

This data confirms that today, if you don't have education, you don't do very well economically. (See Murnane and Levy [1993] for evidence that the disparity in earnings among college graduates, high school graduates, and high school dropouts is continuing, and has become much larger since 1973, partly due to the increased technological demands of work.)

Additional evidence that this is so is the finding, noted earlier, that people in general had substantially less schooling years ago. The high school dropout rate in 1930 was about 50 percent and the median number of years of education completed was ten (Rothstein 1998). In 1910, only about 13.5 percent of the adult population were high school graduates, a figure that increased to 34 percent by 1950. Today (1996), 81 percent of the adult population have graduated high school (Snyder, Hoffman, and Geddes 1996, 17, Table 8).

To be sure, there are academic success stories in many immigrant families. School success, however, did not come first. As Greer (1972) and Steinberg (1989) have pointed out, economic success for immigrant groups preceded school success. This is much less likely to occur today; economic success is much more dependent on school success.

References

Greer, C. 1972. *The Great School Legend.* New York: Viking Press.

McMillen, M., and P. Kaufman. 1997. *Dropout Rates in the United States: 1996.* Washington, DC: U.S. Department of Education NCES.

Murnane, R., and F. Levy. 1993. "Why Today's High-School-Educated Males Earn Less Than Their Fathers Did: The Problem and an Assessment of Responses." *Harvard Educational Review* 63: 1–19.

Olneck, M., and M. Lazerson. 1974. "The School Achievement of Immigrant Children: 1900–1934." *History of Education Quarterly* (winter): 453–482.

Parker, D. 1986. "The Great School Myth: Everybody's Grandfather Made It . . . and Without Bilingual Education." *California Tomorrow* (fall): 16–17.

Rothstein, R. 1998. "Bilingual Education: The Controversy." *Phi Delta Kappan* 79 (9): 672–678.

Rumberger, R. 1983. "Dropping Out of High School: The Influence of Race, Sex, and Family Background." *American Educational Research Journal* 20 (2): 199–220.

———. 1991. "Chicano Dropouts: A Review of Research and Policy Issues." In *Chicano School Failure and Success,* edited by R. Valencia, 64–89. New York: Falmer Press.

———. 1995. "Dropping Out of Middle School: A Multilevel Analysis of Students and Schools." *American Educational Research Journal* 32 (3): 583–625.

Snyder T., C. Hoffman, and C. Geddes. 1996. *Digest of Education Statistics.* Washington, DC: U.S. Department of Education.

Steinberg, S. 1989. *The Ethnic Myth.* Boston: Beacon Press.

U.S. Bureau of the Census. 1997. *Statistical Abstract of the United States: 1997.* (117th edition). Washington, DC.

3

Bogus Argument #3

The United States Is the Only Country That Promotes Bilingual Education

Every other nation uses some form of immersion to teach language to immigrant children; bilingual education is used nowhere else in the world.

—RON UNZ

It has been asserted that bilingual education is done only in the United States, that other countries use only immersion with immigrant children (Unz 1998). Not only is this assertion false, but it is clearly the case that bilingual education has been successful in other countries and that students in bilingual programs acquire the national language as well as or better than students without education in their first language. In the first part of this chapter, I describe instances in which research has been done probing the effectiveness of education in the first language. Much of this research can be criticized: random assignment of students is usually not done, and students in comparison and experimental groups sometimes differ in variables other than the use of the first language. Nevertheless, the results are very positive and consistent.

I present the studies in some detail, as the publications in which they appear may not be easily available to some readers.

Norway

Ozerk (1994) studied the progress of forty-one students, speakers of Turkish, Urdu, and Vietnamese, in Olso, Norway, in a program in which primary language support was available in mathematics, social science, and natural science. All other subjects were done in Norwegian. Because both native speakers of Norwegian and second-language acquirers were in the same classroom, a team-teaching approach was used: a teacher who spoke the child's first language was available for explanation and help in the primary language. Participation was voluntary, but all eligible parents agreed to their child's participation. The team-teaching approach was used from grade 1 to grade 3, and in grade 4, half of the classes were conducted in Norwegian and half with first-language support. Bilingual students were enrolled in four different schools in Oslo.

In this case, the first language was used for only one of the two functions that characterize effective bilingual programs, as hypothesized in Krashen (1996): It was used to provide background knowledge, but was not used for literacy development.

Two comparison groups were used: In the first, twenty-one comparison students, speakers of Turkish, Urdu, Punjabi, Polish, Hindi, Arabic, Indonesian, and Mandarin, were submersed entirely in Norwegian. These students did not have the option of bilingual education because a sufficient number were not enrolled in the same school. These students were enrolled in six different elementary schools in Oslo; four of these schools provided subjects for the bilingual education group. In addition, 108 native speakers of Norwegian constituted a second comparison group. The SES of the two groups of second-language acquirers was identical, but the native speakers were of higher SES.

Ozerk evaluated performance in grades 4 and 5 in mathematics and in social science and natural science, given as a combined score. All tests were given in Norwegian, and possible scores ranged from 1 (highest) to 6 (lowest). Statistical tests confirmed what is clear from Table 3–1: Students in bilingual education significantly outperformed submersion students and were close to the native speakers of Norwegian.

To determine if factors other than participation in bilingual education influenced outcomes, a variety of background variables for the two groups of Norwegian acquirers were studied. Ozerk determined that the following were not significantly related to

Table 3–1
Bilingual Education in Norway

	BILINGUAL EDUCATION GROUP	SUBMERSION GROUP	NATIVE SPEAKERS GROUP
Mathematics			
Grade 4	1.78	3.24	1.57
Grade 5	2.09	3.76	1.71
Social/natural science			
Grade 4	2.12	3.56	1.56
Grade 5	2.59	3.72	1.59

Source: Ozerk (1994)

achievement: gender, length of residence in Norway, parents' educational background, SES, parents' education, and school attendance (bilingual and submersion classes were often in the same school). For all students combined, those students who got more help at home with school work, who used the first language more at home, who went to Norwegian kindergarten, had more social interaction with Norwegian children, and who participated more in organized activities with Norwegian-speaking children did better. But the two groups of Norwegian acquirers did not differ significantly on these variables; there was, in fact, a tendency for submersion students to participate more in Norwegian preschool and kindergarten.

As is nearly always the case, this study is not perfect: Students were not randomly assigned to sections, and there was no control for competence in Norwegian before the children began the program. Nevertheless, there is no reason to hypothesize that the students in the two groups differed in important ways.

England

In Fitzpatrick (1987), sixty-nine Punjabi-speaking children who spoke "little or no" English were randomly assigned to bilingual or all-English preschool programs in two different schools in England. The bilingual program was 50 percent Punjabi and 50 percent English, but it was in some ways similar to the gradual-exit program described in Krashen (1996), with more demanding work done in the first language: "while work in English was typical of work geared to second-language learners, work in Punjabi was planned to make fuller use of the linguistic and conceptual resources at the children's disposal" (53). Due to funding problems, the duration of the project was only one year. The presence of few native speakers of English in the program (in only one of the schools) (51) probably helped to ensure that English input was largely comprehensible for the comparison group as well as for the English portion of the bilingual group's program, but few details are provided.

Children in the bilingual program clearly performed better in tests of Punjabi. Three kinds of measures of oral English were made:

1. Teacher ratings: Ratings of bilingually taught students were slightly higher at month nine, as judged by both monolingual English and bilingual teachers (there were no differences in teacher ratings of English proficiency at the start of the program) (Table 3–2).

2. Oral examinations: Oral examinations were given at the end of the academic year that required speaking and understanding with little contextual help, e.g., children were presented with familiar objects, such as a comb, crayon, and fork, and were asked to tell what was done with an object, describe it, obey commands ("Pick up the spoon."), and so on. Results in one school favored bilingual children in speaking and listening, while results in the second school were split. A follow-up analysis of complex listening tasks only (e.g., "Before you pick up the fork, hand me the pencil.") showed bilingual children to be superior in both schools. Fitzpatrick suggested that the

Table 3–2
Teacher Rating at Month Nine

	BILINGUAL	CONTROL
Monolingual teachers	3.6	3.4
Bilingual teachers	3.6	3.3

Source: Fitzpatrick (1987)

use of the first language promoted the development of what Cummins terms "academic language": "in some way, the experience of the bilingual groups in the bilingual classroom resulted in their being able to perform a complex decoding task in English with a good deal of success. Perhaps the quality of dialogue in Punjabi resulted in the kind of transfer which Cummins talks about . . ." (Fitzpatrick 1987, 87).

3. Follow-up: After the year was over, all children were placed in all-English schools. In follow-up tests done with twenty-seven former bilingual and twenty-one former all-English students eighteen months after the program ended, no differences were found on a variety of measures of English and Punjabi.

Table 3–3
Oral Examination Results: Percentage of Children
Scoring in the Mid to High Range

	KEIGHLEY (%)	BRADFORD (%)
Speaking		
Bilingual	73	48
All-English	59	64
Listening		
Bilingual	72	72
All-English	65	60
"Complex" listening tasks		
Bilingual	47	66
All-English	38	30

Source: Fitzpatrick (1987)

The Netherlands

In Appel (1984; see also Altena and Appel 1982; Appel 1988), twenty-six Turkish and thirty-one Moroccan children ages 7 years to 12.6 years were placed in either bilingual or "regular" classes in Leiden in the Netherlands. Appel reported no initial differences between the groups in the type of neighborhood lived in, TV watching, SES, nonverbal intelligence, or educational level reached by parents in country of origin: "we tried to match the two groups on certain background variables as much as possible" (1984, 35). The mean age of those in the bilingual program was 9.4 years, of the students in the regular program, 9.6 years.

While both groups received special instruction in Dutch for 20 percent of the school day, the bilingual group had all subjects taught in the primary language for the first year, but "as soon as the immigrant children were able to understand and speak some Dutch, they joined Dutch children for a few hours a week in activities (gymnastics, music, and crafts) which were meant to encourage their integration into Dutch life" (30). In the second year, the program was 50 percent primary language and 50 percent Dutch, and in year three all instruction was in Dutch. Table 3–4 presents typical test scores for Dutch language development.

Appel noted that "In general, it can be concluded that the amount of time on minority-language teaching in the transitional bilingual school . . . did not harm or hinder the second-language acquisition of the Turkish and Moroccan immigrant workers' children. At the end of the research period, these children were even somewhat ahead in oral and written second-language proficiency as compared to children who were instructed entirely or almost entirely in Dutch" (50).

The impact of bilingual education was apparently not limited to language: "In the first three school years the mean percentage of 'problem children' in the (regular) group was nearly twice

Table 3–4
Bilingual Versus Nonbilingual Education Students

	AFTER 2 YEARS		FOLLOW-UP ONE YEAR LATER	
	Bil.	Regular	Bil.	Regular
Oral language				
Mean length utterance	4.1	3.8	4.9	4.4
Number of different words produced (measure of vocabulary)	168.1	157.1	213.1	205.9
Picture test (oral)				
Morphology (e.g., plurals)	33.2	34.1	65.9	58.2
Imitation (form sentence from words presented in vertical column)	57.5	50.0	71.5	57.7
Written language				
Cloze test	52.1	51.5	64.3	50.9[a]

[a]$p < .05$

Source: Appel (1984)

as high as in the (bilingual) group (24 percent versus 13 percent). Social-emotional problems were exhibited in aggressive behavior, apathy . . ." (57).

Verhoeven (1991) presents additional data from the Netherlands in a study of 138 "working-class" second-grade Turkish-speaking children. Several groups were studied:

• One group was a "submersion" group. They had instruction only in Dutch in grade 1, with instruction in Turkish literacy "for some hours per week" in grade 2.

- There were two groups of children who had Turkish literacy instruction along with oral Dutch. One subgroup continued with literacy instruction in both languages, adding Dutch after two months, while the other had only Turkish literacy until grade 2. Their scores were combined in the statistical analysis (see Table 3–5, L1 literacy—first subgroup).

- A third group entered the program a year later and also had literacy development in the primary language (see Table 3–5, L1 literacy—second subgroup).

The children who had literacy development in the first language outperformed the "submersion" children in reading comprehension tests in Dutch given at the end of grade 2, although differences were not statistically significant (Table 3–5). (The effect size for the advantage of the first group over the submersion group was a modest .38. For the second group, it was a more substantial .79.)

Much less information is available on a bilingual program in Enschede in the Netherlands. Appel (1988) presents a preliminary report of the progress of Turkish and Moroccan children who had a full bilingual program (56 percent primary language the first year, 44 percent the second; described in Glenn 1996, 460) compared with those who had only a few

Table 3–5
Reading Comprehension in Dutch After Grade 2

GROUP	N	MEAN	SD
L1 literacy—first subgroup	25	13.44	3.6
L1 literacy—second subgroup	38	15.21	4.2
Submersion	74	11.93	4.1

Source: Verhoeven (1991)

hours of first-language instruction per week. Appel reported that bilingual students outperformed comparisons in Dutch reading, and that the Turkish bilingual children approached native speaker norms in reading and even performed above this level two years after leaving the program. Citing Eldering (1983), Glenn (1996), however, notes that in one evaluation, nine out of fourteen Moroccan children (but only one out of seventeen Turkish children) who had done the Enschede program had to repeat grade 3, done in the mainstream (460). We are not told how this compares to the performance of similar children who did not get bilingual education.

Sweden

Lofgren and Ouvinen-Birgerstam (1982) compared the achievement of Finnish-speaking students living in Sweden who participated in a bilingual program to other immigrant children and to native speakers of Swedish. The bilingual program lasted for four years—two years of preschool and two years of elementary school—and included literacy development in the primary language and a gradually increasing component of Swedish language instruction. Subject matter taught in elementary school was done in Swedish in the mainstream, "but with some terms being explained in Finnish" by a teacher; two teachers were present in the class. Immigrant children who spoke other languages had some access to help in their home language, but not nearly as much as the Finnish-speaking children. Children who had bilingual education performed as well as or better than other immigrant children and at the same level in mathematics as native speakers (Table 3–6). While this study suffers from a failure to control for possible preexisting differences among the groups, and lacks a Finnish-speaking control group, the results are certainly suggestive.

Table 3–6
Bilingual Education in Sweden

TEST RESULTS AT GRADE 3	N	SWEDISH (STANDARDIZED TEST)	SWEDISH (GRADE LEVEL)	MATHEMATICS (GRADE LEVEL)
Students				
Finnish	32–34	1.9	2.7	2.9
Other immigrant	29–46	1.9	2.4	2.7
Swedish	33–62	2.3	2.9	2.8

Source: Lofgren and Ouvinen-Birgerstam (1982)

In another study of Finnish-speaking students in Sweden, Hagman and Lahdenpera (1987) reported that graduates of Finnish-Swedish bilingual programs did as well as comparison students (immigrant students from other groups and native speakers of Swedish) in overall school achievement, and there was a tendency for more of the bilingual students to continue to higher education.

Australia

Gale et al. (1981) compared Australian aboriginal children in all-English schools with children who had had bilingual education. The bilingual model presented in Gale et al. taught literacy and subject matter in the primary language (Gapapuyngu), and gradually shifted instruction into English, beginning with math and English literacy. Gapapuyngu language arts were continued until grade 4. When tested in grade 5, there was no difference between the groups in English vocabulary and story retelling (fluency), and the English-only children were better on a cloze test. By grade 7, however, the bilingual education group was significantly better on tests of English fluency, on a cloze test, on English composition, on tests of subtraction, multiplication, and division, and tended to do better in reading. The English-only group was better in vocabulary, but the difference fell short of statistical significance.

As Gale et al. note, the study was not perfect. The English-only controls were previous cohorts, and other curricular developments had been put in place in addition to bilingual education. Also, the community was "becoming more Europeanized" (301), with greater exposure to English. Finally, estimates of validity were not calculated for the locally developed tests (cloze, arithmetic, composition, story retelling; the vocabulary and reading tests were standardized tests). Nevertheless, the results are very strong (Table 3–7).

Table 3–7
Grade 7 Results: Gapapuyngu Study

TEST	ENGLISH ONLY	BILINGUAL	EFFECT SIZE[a]
Vocabulary	51.5	49.5	−.42
Fluency	111.1	132.7	.53
Reading	6.70	7.18	.40
Cloze	24.0	52.5	1.00
Essay	8.8	12.9	1.52

[a]Effect sizes calculated from t-values in Gale et al.

Source: Gale et al. (1981)

Table 3–8
Bilingual Education in Mexico

		CHENALHO	
Percent "able to understand what they read in Spanish"			
Taught in Spanish		66/293 (23%)	
Taught in primary language		49/199 (25%)	
Reading comprehension (Spanish)	N	Mean	S.D.
Taught in Spanish	66	32.9	20.9
Taught in primary language	49	46.1	14.9
Effect size	.71		
		OXCHUC	
Percent "able to understand what they read in Spanish"			
Taught in Spanish		54/367 (15%)	
Taught in primary language		187/460 (41%)	
Reading comprehension (Spanish)	N	Mean	S.D.
Taught in Spanish	54	47.2	16.8
Taught in primary language	187	50.8	18.4
Effect size	.20		

Mexico

Modiano (1968) describes a program in which children were either taught to read in their primary language (Tzeltal or Tzotzil) or in the second language (Spanish) in special classes designed to prepare children for the first grade, which is done entirely in Spanish. Children taught to read in the first language attended

Table 3–8
continued

		ZINACANTAN	
Percent "able to understand what they read in Spanish"			
Taught in Spanish		45/152 (30%)	
Taught in primary language		54/130 (42%)	
Reading comprehension (Spanish)	N	Mean	S.D.
Taught in Spanish	45	47.6	15.0
Taught in primary language	54	52.5	22.3
Effect size	.25		

Source: Modiano (1968)

bilingual schools of the National Indian Institute, while those taught in Spanish attended state-sponsored schools. The schools, however, were "matched as closely as possible on the basis of demographic data for the hamlets they served" (35).

Modiano reported that children who learned to read in their primary language were significantly more likely to be selected by teachers as being able to understand what they read in Spanish and significantly outperformed comparison children on a test of reading comprehension. Table 3–8 presents the results for students in three separate areas of Mexico.

China

Lin (1997) notes that Korean speakers in China (Yuanbian prefecture in Northern Jiln) have had a great deal of success with bilingual education. Lin concludes that as a result of their well-designed and well-supported bilingual program, "the Koreans are the highest achievers in education, exceeding the level of the Han overall" (202). They have a very low dropout rate, and the percentage of Korean speakers in higher education is three times the national average. Of course, without a comparison group, it is difficult to know whether bilingual education should receive full credit for these accomplishments, but such results certainly suggest that use of the first language in school does no harm.

Comments on Experimental Design

Taken as a group, the studies from other countries are remarkably consistent. In no case do children educated using their home language do worse than comparison children, and they usually do better. As noted in the descriptions of the studies, however, the individual studies have flaws.

Duration: It has been observed that the impact of education in the primary language sometimes takes time before it is obvious in test scores. The studies included here were of modest duration: Fitzpatrick (1987) and Modiano (1968) lasted only one year; Verhoeven (1991) and Appel (1984) two years, Ozerk (1994) three years, and Lofgren and Ouvinen-Birgerstam (1982) and Gale et al. (1981) four years.

Control for preexisting differences: To be sure that subjects in different groups do not differ from each other before the beginning of the study, researchers either randomly assign subjects to experimental and control groups or use statistical techniques to control for possible differences. It is widely agreed that randomization is the best way of doing this. Only Fitzpatrick (1987) used random assignment, and none of the other studies employed statistical means for dealing with preexisting differences. Appel

(1984), however, attempted to "match the two groups on certain background variables as much as possible" as noted earlier, and the children studied in Modiano (1968) came from similar backgrounds. I have argued (Krashen 1996) that this flaw is not fatal: We have no reason to suspect that important differences existed between groups, and results are consistent over many studies. In Krashen (1996) I concluded that of a set of twelve studies that did not control for preexisting differences, ten were supportive of bilingual education, one showed no difference, and none were negative. We can now add Ozerk (1994) and Appel (1984) to this set of positive studies that did not control for preexisting differences (the other studies discussed in this paper were included in Krashen 1996). Such consistent results cannot be ignored.

Definition of bilingual education: I have argued (Krashen 1996) that in some cases in which immersion was claimed to be better than bilingual education, neither term was well defined. "Immersion" was sometimes used to refer to programs that were really bilingual, and "bilingual" programs were sometimes poorly set up. In the set of studies considered here, comparison children had little or no help in the primary language, and bilingual education appears to be done in a way that is consistent with the framework discussed in Krashen (1996): The first language is used for literacy development in all cases except for Ozerk (1994) and appears to be used for subject matter teaching in several cases (not in Modiano [1968]; minimally in Lofgren and Ouvinen-Birgerstam [1982]; information is lacking in Verhoeven [1991]). In addition, instruction in and through the second language is increased gradually. None of the studies appeared to use translation models.

Appropriate comparison group: Ideally, comparison groups should be similar to the experimental group. In some studies, however, comparison groups did not speak the same home language, but were composed of immigrant children who spoke other home languages (Lofgren and Ouvinen-Birgerstam 1982; Ozerk 1994).

Use of statistical tests: Ideally, researchers should use appropriate statistical tests to determine whether groups were significantly different from each other, and should compute effect sizes to determine the magnitude of the difference between the groups (e.g., Wolf 1986). Availability of effect-size data makes it possible to perform a meta-analysis, which gives us a quantified summary of a group of studies. Statistical tests were done in the studies reviewed here, but effect sizes were not calculated. Based on the data provided by the researchers, I was only able to calculate effect sizes for three studies—Verhoeven (1991), Gale et al. (1981), and Modiano (1968).

The "flaws" in the design of the studies reviewed here are in general a result of experimenters' working under severe constraints. It is rarely possible to randomly assign children into groups, and one must often work with the groups one has available. Most important, the results are very robust, and different studies have different flaws.

Table 3–9
Summary of Studies

COUNTRY	FIRST LANGUAGE	RESULTS
Norway	Turkish, Urdu Vietnamese	L1 support in math, social sciences, natural science, grades 1–4; BE students better than controls in math,

Table 3–9
continued

COUNTRY	FIRST LANGUAGE	RESULTS
		social/natural science in grades 4, 5, perform close to native speakers of Norwegian (Ozerk 1994).
England	Punjabi	Preschool 50 percent Punjabi. BE same or better in English fluency (Fitzpatrick 1987).
Netherlands (Leiden)	Turkish, Arabic	Bilingual students taught all in primary language for 1st year with Dutch as second language, 50 percent 2d year. At end of 3d year, outperform controls in Dutch language, fewer behavioral problems, had more social relations with Dutch children (Appel 1984).
Netherlands	Turkish	Bilingual students outperform control students in Dutch literacy in grade 2; differences not statistically significant (Verhoeven 1991).
Sweden	Finnish	At grade 3, students outperform controls (speakers of other languages) (Lofgren and Ouvinen-Birgerstam 1982).
Sweden	Finnish	Graduates of bilingual programs do as well as controls (includes native speakers) in school achievement, slightly more continue to higher education than controls after grade 9 (Hagman and Lahdenpera 1987).
Australia	Gapapuyngu	Bilinguals outperform controls in grade 7 in math, English

continues

Table 3–9

continued

COUNTRY	FIRST LANGUAGE	RESULTS
		composition, tend to be better in English reading (Gale et al. 1981)
Mexico	Tzeltal,Tzotzil	Reading taught in vernacular during preparatory year results in better Spanish reading (Modiano 1968).
China	Korean	Full bilingual programs; more Korean speakers obtain higher education degrees than native speakers of Mandarin (Lin 1997).

Less convincing, but nevertheless impressive evidence is the fact that so many countries do some form of bilingual education. In the following list, I present the countries and the languages involved. All are state-supported.[1]

Programs with intensive first-language instruction have been described for children of immigrants in Bavaria in Germany. Some children are placed in all-German programs with supplementary instruction in the home language for eight lessons per week (home language enrichment, see below) while those with less knowledge of German receive all their instruction in their home language, with German taught as a foreign language for eight periods per week, with German also used in art, music, and physical education (Nist 1978, 210). The goal of the latter program was "to bring the foreign child to a level of proficiency whereby he/she can choose to continue in the mother-tongue classroom or move to a German-language classroom" (211). Such programs also exist in the Netherlands for Turkish and Moroccan children (Vallen and Stijnen 1987), in Sweden for Finnish, Swedish, Turkish, Serbocroatan, Greek, and Arabic children (Hagman and Lahdenpera 1987), and in several countries for indigenous minorities: For the Basques in Spain (Cummins 1993; Arzamendi and Genesee 1997), for the Inuit in Canada (Stairs 1988), and for Quechua and Aymara speakers in Peru (Hornberger 1987, 1988), and were established for speakers of minority languages in the former Soviet Union (Kreusler 1961). In China, "by 1995, twenty-three minority groups (Mongolians, Tibetans, Koreans, Uygar, and Zhuang, among others) were using their own language, or both their own language and Mandarin, to teach" (Lin 1997, 195).

Glenn (1996) describes a variety of programs for immigrant children in a number of countries. "Bilingual reception programs" are designed for students "arriving beyond the usual school-entry age" and "make use of the home language of pupils to ease their adjustment and speed their learning of language and other skills considered necessary before they are mainstreamed" (452). Such programs exist in Belgium (Arabic, Turkish), Germany (Turkish), and the Netherlands (Arabic, Berber, Turkish).[2]

In "integrated bilingual" programs "language minority and majority students learn together, with a carefully crafted emphasis on both languages" (461), similar to two-way programs in the United States. Such programs exist in Denmark (Turkish), Belgium (Spanish), Sweden (Finnish), and Germany (Turkish, Greek). Integrated bilingual programs are also available in the Netherlands for Frisian, the language spoken in Friesland, a part of the Netherlands (Vallen and Stijnen 1987; Zondag 1989), and Denmark provides German/Danish integrated bilingual schooling for its German-speaking minority in the Jutland area. Sondergaard and Byram (1986) report that 22 percent of the students in these schools report German as their only home language. Gerth (1988) reports that in the north of France, "French and immigrants' children, from Portugal or Algeria or Morocco or Italy, are put together in the same class. They all get about six hours a week in that foreign—or native—language. All subjects can be taught in that language as far as the teachers' work is related to the official French syllabus" (200).

"Home language enrichment" programs were often originally designed to help guestworkers and their families reintegrate into their original homelands but continue for those who are clearly permanent residents. These are often after-school programs, but are occasionally integrated into the school day; in France, for example, home language enrichment is provided for three hours per week as part of the school day, and in the Netherlands the law allows for two and a half hours per week of home language enrichment during the school day and two and a half hours after school per week. State-supported home language instruction is provided in Australia (Italian, Dutch, Hebrew, Ukrainian, Lithuanian, Greek, Latvian, Polish, Hungarian, Vietnamese, and Turkish, among others), Belgium (Arabic), Canada (Chinese, Greek, German, Italian, and Ukrainian), Denmark (Arabic, Turkish, Serbocroatian, Greek; according to Pavlinic-Wolf, Brcic, and Jeftic, "in the school year 1985–86, mother-tongue instruction in Copenhagen was organized for the speakers of twenty-five non-Danish languages" [1988, 152]), France (Italian, Arabic, Spanish, Serbocroatian, Turkish, Portuguese; see also Gerth [1988], who reports that Catalan, Basque, and Breton are taught in French schools in certain areas for three hours per week), Germany (Turkish), the Netherlands (Turkish, Spanish, Portuguese, Italian, Arabic), Sweden (Spanish, Arabic), and the United Kingdom (Punjabi, Cantonese, Italian, Bengali). In addition, Darnell and Hoem (1996) describe schools for Saami-speaking children in Sweden, largely in Swedish but with instruction in Saami language and culture, and in Norway, using the Saami language as the language of instruction.

Another category is language revival programs, in which curriculum is taught in a language that few in the community speak. Their design is similar to Canadian French immersion programs.

They exist in New Zealand for Maori (Shafer 1988; Cazden 1989; Benton 1989), in Canada for Ukrainian (Muller et al. 1977), and in English-speaking Wales in Welsh (Thomas 1991, Macnamara 1967).

If one expands the definition of bilingual education even more, one could include situations such as Hong Kong, where both Cantonese and English are widely used; while clearly a Cantonese-speaking city, 27 percent claimed that they knew English "quite well" in 1993, up from 5 percent in 1983 (Bacon-Shone and Bolton 1998). Primary education has been in Cantonese in Hong Kong, with most students attending English medium schools at higher levels; in the last two decades, both Cantonese and English have been used in higher education with texts in English and oral instruction in Cantonese or both (Boyle 1997; Johnston 1998). Similarly, one could include schools in the Catalan-speaking areas of Spain that teach in Catalan, with Spanish introduced by grade 3; Catalan/Spanish bilingual programs also exist for native speakers of Spanish living in these areas, with all instruction in Catalan for the first two to five years (Artigal 1997) as well as Basque-Spanish bilingual schools in the Basque-speaking areas of Spain, which service native speakers of both Basque and Spanish (Arzamendi and Genesee 1997).

This survey does not include "immersion" programs, which are "bilingual" in that two languages are used for subject matter instruction, but one is actually a foreign language. Originally done in English-speaking Canada for French, they are now in operation in several other countries, including the United States (Johnson and Swain 1997).

Notes

1. See also Gorter (1991), who reported that the Fyske Academy in the Netherlands presented a report on the status of minority language communities in Europe, including Basque (Spain and France), Catalan

(Spain, France, and Italy), German (Italy, Belgium, Denmark), Irish (Ireland), Danish (Netherlands), French (Italy), Frisian (Netherlands), Galician (Spain), Letseburgish (Luxembourg), Slovenian (Italy), Welsh (United Kingdom), Sardinian (Italy), Breton (France), Corsican (France), German (France), Ladin (Italy), Occitan (France), Scottish Gaelic (United Kingdom), Albanian (Italy), Cornish (United Kingdom), Croatian (Italy), Flemish (France), Friulian (Italy), North Frisian (Germany), Irish (Northern Ireland), Occitan (Italy), East Frisian (Germany), and Romani (Italy). All but three minority languages (East Frisian, Sardinian, and Romani) are taught in primary education in the European Economic Community and none are forbidden by law in the EEC: No member of the European Economic Community has passed the equivalent of California's Proposition 227.

2. During the recent Proposition 227 discussion in California, critics of bilingual education frequently used the case of Israel as an example of success without bilingual education. Israel, the argument went, does not do bilingual education but has a Hebrew-only intensive language training policy that is very successful. According to a report in the *Los Angeles Times*, however (Miller 1998), there is no research on immigrant success in Israel, and educators in Israel conclude that "the immigrants' success is uneven at best," with Russians from better-educated families typically doing better than immigrants from Ethiopia, whose parents are often illiterate. The dropout rate among Ethiopians who arrived during the 1980s and 1990s, according to Miller, is higher than that of other groups. Thus, Russian immigrant children may have had de facto bilingual education (Krashen 1996), with literacy and subject matter knowledge supplied through the first language outside of school.

Interestingly, Israel is now experimenting with bilingual education. Miller reports that "there is a pilot program to teach Ethiopians first in their native Amharic and then in Hebrew." In addition, the Ministry of Education issued a document on April 15, 1996, with policy to take effect in September, 1996, that includes "language maintenance in the languages of immigrants, with special reference to Russian and Amharic" (Spolsky and Shohamy 1996).

References

Altena, N., and R. Appel. 1982. "Mother Tongue Teaching and the Acquisition of Dutch by Turkish and Morrocan Immigrant Workers' Children." *Journal of Multilingual and Multicultural Development* 3 (4): 315–332.

Appel, R. 1984. *Immigrant Children Learning Dutch.* Dordrecht, The Netherlands: Foris.

———. 1988. "The Language Education of Immigrant Workers' Children in the Netherlands." In *Minority Education: From Shame to Struggle,* edited by T. Skutnabb-Kangas and J. Cummins. Clevedon, UK: Multilingual Matters.

Artigal, J. 1997. "The Catalan Immersion Program." In *Immersion Education: International Perspectives,* edited by K. Johnson and M. Swain. Cambridge: Cambridge University Press.

Arzamendi, J., and F. Genesee. 1997. "Reflections on Immersion Education in the Basque Country." In *Immersion Education: International Perspectives,* edited by K. Johnson and M. Swain. Cambridge: Cambridge University Press.

Bacon-Shone, J.Ï, and K. Bolton. 1998. "Charting Multilingualism: Language Censuses and Language Surveys in Hong Kong." In *Language in Hong Kong at Century's End,* edited by M. Pennington. Hong Kong: Hong Kong University Press.

Benton, N. 1989. "Education, Language Decline and Language Revitalization: The Case of Maori in New Zealand." *Language and Education* 3 (2): 65–82.

Boyle, J. 1997. "The Use of Mixed-Code Teaching in Hong Kong English Language Teaching." *System 25* (1): 83–89.

Cazden, C. 1989. "Richmond Road: A Multilingual, Multicultural Primary School in Auckland, New Zealand." *Language and Education* 3 (3): 143–166.

Clyne, M. 1991. "Immersion Principles in Second Language Programs— Research and Policy in Multicultural Australia." *Journal of Multilingual and Multicultural Development* 12 (1, 2): 55–65.

Cummins, J. 1993. "Bilingualism and Second Language Learning." *Annual Review of Applied Linguistics* 13: 51–70.

Darnell, F., and A. Hoem. 1996. *Taken to Extremes: Education in the Far North.* Olso: Scandinavian University Press.

Engle, P. 1975. "Language Medium in Early School Years for Minority Language Groups." *Review of Educational Research* 45 (2): 283–325.

Fitzpatrick, F. 1987. *The Open Door.* Clevedon, UK: Multilingual Matters.

Gale, K., D. McClay, M. Christie, and S. Harris. 1981. "Academic Achievement in the Milingimbi Bilingual Education Program." *TESOL Quarterly* 15: 297–314.

Gerth, K-E. 1988. "Latest Developments in Early Bilingual Education in France and Southern Europe." *Journal of Multilingual and Multicultural Education* 9 (1, 2): 193–202.

Glenn, C. 1996. *Educating Immigrant Children.* New York: Garland Publishers.

Gorter, D. 1991. "Lesser Used Languages in Primary Education in the European Community." In *Ethnic Minority Languages and Education,* edited by K. Jaspaert and S. Kroon. Amsterdam: Swets and Zeitlinger.

Hagman, T., and J. Lahdenpera. 1987. "Nine Years of Finnish-Medium Education in Sweden." In *Minority Education: From Shame to Struggle,* edited by T. Skutnabb-Kangas and J. Cummins. Clevedon, UK: Multilingual Matters.

Hornberger, N. 1987. "Bilingual Education and Quechua Language Maintenance in Highland Puno, Peru." *NABE Journal* 11 (2): 117–140.

———. 1988. "Misbehavior, Punishment and Put-Down: Stress for Quechua Children in School." *Language and Education* 2 (4): 239–253.

Johnston, R., 1998. "Language and Education in Hong Kong." In *Language in Hong Kong at Century's End,* edited by M. Pennington. Hong Kong: Hong Kong University Press.

Johnson, R., and M. Swain. 1997. *Immersion Education: International Perspectives.* Cambridge: Cambridge University Press.

Krashen, S. 1996. *Under Attack: The Case Against Bilingual Education.* Culver City, CA: Language Education Associates.

Kruesler, A. 1961. "Bilingualism in Soviet Non-Russian Schools." *Elementary School Journal* 62: 94–99.

Lin, J. 1997. "Policies and Practices of Bilingual Education for the Minorities of China." *Journal of Multilingual and Multicultural Development* 18 (3): 193–205.

Lofgren, H., and P. Ouvinen-Birgerstam. 1982. "A Bilingual Model for the Teaching of Immigrant Children." *Journal of Multilingual and Multicultural Development* 3 (4): 323–331.

Macnamara, J. 1967. "The Effects of Instruction in a Weaker Language." *Journal of Social Issues* 23 (2): 121–135.

Miller, M. 1998. "Israel's Success in Teaching Hebrew Linked to Ideology." *Los Angeles Times,* 30 May.

Modiano, N. 1968. "National or Mother Tongue Language in Beginning Reading: A Comparative Study." *Research in the Teaching of English* 2: 32–43.

Muller, L., W. Penner, T. Blowers, J. Jones, and H. Mosychuk. 1977. "Evaluation of a Bilingual (English-Ukranian) Program." *Canadian Modern Language Review* 33: 475–485.

Nist, R. 1978. *Guestworkers in Germany: The Prospects for Pluralism.* New York: Praeger Publishers.

Ozerk, K. 1994. "Subject Matter Acquisition and Language Development." In *University of Olso Pedagogiskforskningsinstitutt, Report Number 3,* edited by S. Ozerk. Oslo: University of Oslo.

Pavlinic-Wolf, A., K. Brcic, and N. Jeftic. 1988. "Supplementary Mother-Tongue Education and the Linguistic Development of Yugoslav Children in Denmark." *Journal of Multilingual and Multicultural Development* 9 (1, 2): 151–176.

Shafer, S. 1988. "Bilingual/Bicultural Education for Maori Cultural Preservation in New Zealand." *Journal of Multilingual Multicultural Development* 9 (6) 487–501.

Sondergaard, B., and M. Byram. 1986. "Pedagogical Problems and Symbolic Values in the Language Curriculum—The Case of the German Minority in Denmark." *Journal of Multilingual and Multicultural Development* 7 (2, 3): 147–167.

Spolsky, B., and E. Shohamy. 1996. *National Profiles of Languages in Education: Israel: Language Policy.* Bar Ilan University: Language Policy Research Center.

Stairs, A. 1988. "Beyond Cultural Inclusion." In *Minority Language: From Shame to Struggle,* edited by T. Skutnabb-Kangas and J. Cummins. Clevedon, UK: Multilingual Matters.

Thomas, P. 1991. "Children in Welsh-Medium Education: Semilinguals or Innovators?" *Journal of Multilingual and Multicultural Development* 12 (1, 2): 45–53.

Unz, R. 1998. Presentation at California State University, Northridge, March, 1998.

Vallen, T., and S. Stijnen. 1987. "Language and Educational Success of Indigenous and Non-Indigenous Minority Students in the Netherlands." *Language and Education* 1 (2):109–124.

Verhoeven, L. 1991. "Acquisition of Biliteracy." *AILA Review* 8: 61–74.

Wolf, F. 1986. *Meta-Analysis.* Thousand Oaks, CA: Sage Publications.

Zondag, K. 1989. "Diversity and Uniformity in Six Bilingual Schools in Friesland." *Journal of Multilingual and Multicultural Development* 10 (1): 3–16.

4

Bogus Argument #4

Bilingual Education Failed in California

The evidence has been mounting for years that bilingual education is a poor way for children to learn English. . . . Bilingual education's documented failures, particularly as measured by standardized tests in specific school districts, make it a ripe target. What's more, school systems have refused even to test many children in bilingual programs, making it easier to hide the programs' failures.

—R. CLEGG

The "failure" of bilingual education has reached the status of urban myth. Even those who were opposed to California's Proposition 227 assumed that bilingual education had serious problems. The research, however, does not say this at all. Some reviewers of research comparing bilingual education to alternative programs conclude that bilingual education has been a true success, that children in properly organized bilingual programs impressively and consistently outperform those in English-only programs (Cummins 1981; Krashen and Biber 1988; Krashen 1996). Others have concluded that bilingual programs provide a slight advantage over all-English alternatives (Willig 1985; Greene 1998), but Willig concludes that the effect of bilingual education is stronger when the research design is better, and both Willig and Greene examine the effect of short-term studies in which the term "bilingual education" is not carefully defined. Rossell and Baker's (1996) conclusions are by far the most negative, and their methodology has been criticized in Krashen (1996), but their conclusion is that while "structured immersion" appears to be more effective, "additional, methodologically sound research needs to be conducted in order for the courts and policymakers to make intelligent decisions" (39). Rossell (1998), in fact, concludes that "bilingual education is a little bit worse than a structured-immersion classroom." The range represented here is from enthusiastic support for bilingual education to a conclusion that bilingual education is a little worse than alternatives, and that more research is necessary. This is hardly a collection of "documented failures."

Some critics admit that the research is not all that negative, but point to problems in application. Two kinds of complaints are frequent: Children, it is claimed, who speak English better than the home language, or whose parents demand all-English instruction, are inappropriately placed in bilingual classes, children and schools have refused to allow them out of the programs. A second complaint is that students languish in bilingual programs for years, and never learn enough English to survive in the mainstream. It is hard to determine how prevalent misplacement and "languishing" are. In the case of misplacement, all we know is that a few cases have been widely publicized in the national media. In the case of languishing, no data that I know of has ever been published. In fact, studies show that by the time children in bilingual education programs are in the third grade, they are doing 75 percent of their subject matter work in English (Mitchell, Destino, and Karan 1997).

To be sure, inappropriate practice may exist, but without empirical evidence it is premature to condemn bilingual education. Most important, even if such inappropriate practice did exist, the first step should certainly be to eliminate the practice, rather than eliminating bilingual education. If we discovered cases of poor algebra teaching (which certainly must exist), we would not conclude that we must stop teaching algebra.

I examine here some cases that have been declared victories for all-English programs over bilingual education. Some have received extensive publicity in the press during the Proposition 227 campaign in California. Closer inspection shows that these cases contain no evidence whatsoever against bilingual education.

Westminster School District: Did They Drop Bilingual Education?

The Westminster School District claimed that it achieved success without bilingual education. In an article in the *Long Island News-day* with the title "Booting Bilingual Education" (Elias 1997), it was claimed that "after 18 months of instruction only in English . . . pupils have made better academic progress and learned more English than they did when taught in their native languages."

There are two serious problems with this claim: (1) One cannot claim the current program is better than bilingual education: Westminster never had a full bilingual program and actually increased the amount of first-language support it provided. (2) The gains made by LEP children in Westminster in the year studied were modest, and no comparison was made with any previous programs.

What changes actually occurred in Westminster? According

to language census data gathered by the State of California, Westminster dramatically changed its services to LEP students in recent years, *but has not reduced bilingual education;* in fact, it *increased* the amount of first-language support it gives its LEP children. In addition, more children in Westminster are now getting SDAI (Specially Designed Academic Instruction, i.e., content taught in English in a comprehensible way for limited English proficient students), more are getting first-language support through paraprofessionals, and substantially more are getting services of some kind:

YEAR	ESL ONLY (%)	ESL/ SDAI (%)	L1 SUPPORT (%)	BIL. ED. (%)	NO SERVICES (%)	TOTAL N
1997	0	34	57	2	7	4,176
1993	34	0	28	0	38	3,456

According to Tracy Painter, Westminster director of special projects, the impetus for applying for a waiver of bilingual classes in 1995 was not a rejection of bilingual education, but was because of a shortage of teachers who spoke Vietnamese: About half of the LEP children in the district are Vietnamese speakers (Elias 1997).

Recent reports confirm that help in the primary language is currently provided by bilingual teaching assistants. In an article in the *Los Angeles Times,* Nguyen (1997) quotes Painter as saying that "our programs could not succeed without our bilingual instructional assistants." In one second-grade class described by Nguyen, in which seventeen of nineteen students are Vietnamese speakers, a Vietnamese-speaking teaching assistant "spends $17\frac{1}{2}$ hours a week in the class, where he speaks Vietnamese to explain concepts to small groups of students." Thus, it is clear that Westminster never had a full Vietnamese bilingual program because of the teacher shortage, and is doing a reduced form of bilingual education with teaching assistants.

Progress in English Reading

Westminster compared English reading results in spring of 1997 to those in spring of 1996 (Westminster School District 1997); this comparison thus measured growth of children in the academic year 1996–1997. (The 1996 program in Westminster was similar to the 1997 program described above: 12 percent of the LEP students were in ESL only, 30 percent in SDAI, 57 percent had first language support, and 1 percent were described as being in a full bilingual program.)

Westminster claimed that their LEP students had increased their scores three NCE points, from the 27th to the 30th percentile. This calculation was based on students who had taken the test both times, spring 1996 and spring 1997—1,588 children out of an LEP population of 4,176 children (29 percent). Gains in language were similar, from the 35th percentile to the 38th percentile. These gains are not impressive. At this rate, it would take the children another seven years to reach the 50th percentile in reading, and another four to reach national norms in language.

Westminster also claimed that 76 percent of the LEP children progressed at least one level on the IPT measure of English oral fluency, a test with seven levels, but Westminster only included gains on the first five levels in their analysis. The average gain was 1.1 level (Westminster School District 1997). Thus, one-quarter of the LEP children in Westminster failed to make measurable progress in oral English in a one-year period! Unfortunately, we do not know what the average gain was on these measures under the previous program. We have no idea how well Westminster LEP children performed in 1993, for example, compared to 1997. All we know is that LEP children made very modest gains in one year under the new program.

Can we interpret this data as showing that the new "bilingual" program is not effective? Unfortunately, there is very little we can conclude. The new program relies on paraprofessionals, not qualified bilingual teachers, to provide first-language support: We do not have real details on its implementation (some models of bilingual education are more effective than others), and many other crucial factors (e.g., the print environment), are not described. From the reports in the newspapers, it appears that literacy is not provided in the first language, nor is there direct subject matter instruction through the first language—factors considered crucial to successful bilingual education. Finally, there is no data comparing achievement under the old and new programs. All we can really conclude about Westminster is that conclusions about improvement after a rejection of bilingual education have been inaccurate.

The Taft School

> Matta Tuchman says Taft shows what other schools could do if allowed to convert to English immersion. (Anderson 1997, A18)

Children at the Taft School in Santa Ana scored at the 48th percentile in English reading on the CTBS in spring of 1997, well above the district average of 22.5 and the highest in the district. Taft's principal credited the school's English immersion philosophy for some of this performance (*Education Week*, 14 January 1998).

Los Angeles Times reporter Nick Anderson, however, noted that Taft "has some demographic advantages. About 36 percent of Taft students are classified as 'limited English proficient,' less than half the average for Santa Ana elementary schools. The campus also draws from a neighborhood more prosperous than the city as a whole" (1997, A18).

The *L.A. Times* published reading comprehension scores for each of the thirty-one schools in the Santa Ana district, along with the percentage of children in each school eligible for reduced or free lunch (a proxy for socioeconomic class), and the percentage of children classified as limited English proficient. The district means, calculated from the *L.A. Times'* data, are presented below, with standard deviations in parentheses:

	CTBS READING, GRADE 5	% FREE/ REDUCED LUNCH	% LEP
District	22.5 (11.09)	80.1 (17.9)	77.8 (20.1)
Taft	48	43.8	36.2

This data confirms Anderson's observation that Taft has demographic advantages. Taft lies two standard deviations above the mean for free/reduced lunch as well as for percent of limited English proficient students.

Correlational analysis confirms that these variables are very strongly related: Schools with higher reading scores had fewer children on free/reduced lunch and fewer LEP children. These results are similar to those reported in Krashen (1996), in which exit rates for Los Angeles clusters were closely related to socioeconomic factors.

	CTBS READING	% OF STUDENTS WITH FREE/ REDUCED LUNCH
% free/reduced lunch	−.926	
% LEP	−.946	.960

There are several reasons why socioeconomic factors are strongly related to literacy development, other than the superior material benefits that accompany economic advantages. The first is the print environment. It is well established that the availability of print and reading scores are closely related (Krashen 1993) and that more advantaged children have more access to print at home and at school (McQuillan 1998; Smith, Constantino, and Krashen 1997). Second, higher SES children are more likely to have had quality education before coming to the United States. They have had, in other words, de facto bilingual education (Krashen 1996): Subject matter knowledge and literacy development in the primary language, two of the three components of quality bilingual education programs. The powerful influence of economics found here does not, therefore, negate the value of bilingual education; it is consistent with the view that providing good education in the first language is an advantage.

It would be of value to include in such an analysis the impact of bilingual education programs. Unfortunately, this data was not provided, other than the knowledge that bilingual education is not done at Taft. It is ". . . an English-immersion oasis . . ." (Anderson 1997, A16).

Regression analysis shows that Taft's reading score is accurately predicted by socioeconomic factors: The following regression equation was computed, based on the *Los Angeles Times*' data:

Reading score = 68.6 − .576 (% on free/reduced lunch)

Taft's predicted score, according to this equation, is 43.3. Taft's actual score, 48, is not significantly larger than the predicted score (standard error of the estimate = 4.25), which means that the lack of a bilingual education program at Taft did not make a difference: It did not help and it did not hurt.

Taft's "success" has, most likely, nothing to do with the absence of bilingual education. In fact, some of it could be due to de facto bilingual education, the superior education in the primary language that more advantaged children tend to have.

Orange Unified School District

An article in the Orange County edition of the *Los Angeles Times* announced on April 18, 1998, that "A controversial new English immersion program in the Orange Unified School District appears to help many students learn to speak the language faster than traditional bilingual programs, according to a preliminary report" (Wright 1998). The article announced that "almost a quarter of the district's 4,132 elementary students in the immersion program had advanced their fluency by at least one level in the first five months of study." Orange dropped bilingual education the year before and "went with English immersion."

The problems with this analysis are identical to those we saw in Westminster, discussed earlier: An inspection of the program currently used in Orange reveals considerable use of the first language; no comparison was made with earlier versions of bilingual education; and the gains are not that extraordinary. The full report on Orange was made available to me by the consultant who wrote it, Kevin Clark.

While Orange claimed that they eliminated bilingual education, in reality their new English immersion program was a version of bilingual education that is very hard to implement; preview/review, a technique that calls for a delicate balance of first-language and second-language input. The first-language instructor is supposed to provide just enough to make the English portion comprehensible. Ideally, there should be no repetition of content, to avoid wasting time and to avoid boredom. First-language use was limited to about thirty minutes per day.

Apparently, bilingual instructional assistants are responsible for the first-language component in Orange Unified (Clark 1998, 21). Thus, paraprofessionals are not only being used as teachers, they are being asked to be experts, providing just enough background in the first language to make subsequent input in English comprehensible.

The use of the first language in this way, to provide background knowledge that makes English input more comprehensible, is quite consistent with the theory presented in Krashen (1996), but it is a very hard way to do it.

To understand what progress was made in English (only oral English was investigated in Clark's study), we need to refer to the following stages in oral development, used in Clark's report (Krashen and Terrell 1983):

1. preproduction
2. early production
3. speech emergence
4. intermediate fluency
5. redesignation

It is hypothesized that when children reach stage 3, speech emergence, they know enough English to be able to understand the modified language used in at least some sheltered subject matter teaching ("It is generally accepted that students of speech emergent and intermediate fluency can access a good deal of grade appropriate content area instruction in English as long as that instruction is modified by the teacher" [Clark 1998, 29]). To be able to understand language use in the mainstream, attainment of at least stage 4 is necessary, although many would assume that stage 5 is necessary. These hypotheses are, however, hypotheses, without, as far as I know, empirical bases, and do not consider the specific subject matter involved.

The following table summarizes the results of Clark's evaluation and includes his estimates of what is expected of children at each level, based on other research (this research was not cited in his report, however):

MOVEMENT FROM STAGE	TIME FRAME: "MOST RESEARCH"	TIME FRAME ORANGE COUNTY
1 to 2	0–6 mos.	4 mos. (43%)
2 to 3	6 mos.–1 year	4 mos. (40%)
3 to 4	1–3 years	4 mos. (17%)

Being as generous as possible, assuming that stage 3 is enough for some sheltered subject matter instruction, and that stage 4 is enough for the mainstream, the data show that about 40 percent of the children will move from stages 1 to 3 in one year and be ready for some sheltered subject matter instruction in English, and that 17 percent will reach the rock-bottom level to understand mainstream classes in 1.5 years. (If we accept stage 5 as the minimum for the mainstream, the outlook is bleaker, as only 2 percent of the children moved from stage 4 to 5 in the four-month period studied.)

Again, no comparison was made with a full bilingual program. All we can conclude is that gains in oral English competence took place. No miracles occurred, and the results confirm that it takes quite a while to develop enough English to do work in the mainstream. Wright's conclusion that English immersion was shown to be an improvement over bilingual education was completely unfounded.

Evergreen Elementary School District

> I'm surprised educators don't seem to know much about alternatives to bilingual education used in Evergreen and Cupertino elementary districts. Both districts spent years developing English-language models. Both show excellent results.' (Jacobs 1998)

The situation in Evergreen Elementary School District is very similar to what we have seen elsewhere: the first language is used to some extent, and there is no comparison with bilingual education.

The Evergreen District clearly has an English-emphasis program, with "whole language instruction" from the classroom teacher in kindergarten and grades 1 and 2, and English language development continues throughout elementary school, either by the classroom teacher or as ESL pull-out. However, some academic support in the primary language is made available through paraprofessionals. Evergreen provides data on the success of children who have been reclassified; these children are clearly doing well, but we are not told how long it took them to achieve their current level. All we are told is that all were once classified as LEP for a period of at least one year. No comparison is made with similar children in full bilingual programs.

Evergreen also notes that about 20 percent of its LEP population is reclassified every year. Again, it is hard to come to firm conclusions here, as no comparison is made with other programs, and reclassification rates are strongly correlated with socioeconomic factors (Krashen 1996).

Los Angeles Unified School District

Another reported case of the failure of bilingual education has its origins in an article published in the *Los Angeles Times* on March 2, 1998. The results of an initial report looked very good for bilingual education: Spanish-speaking children who had been in bilingual programs for five years were compared to those who had not been placed in bilingual education and participated in an English language development program. All children began as LEP in kindergarten or first grade. The children in the bilingual program outperformed those not in bilingual education on Stanford 9 tests of English language, administered in English. Fourth-grade CTBS results with the same students showed a similar pattern.

The *Times* article revealed, however, that while nearly all of the children not in bilingual education took the test, a substantial number of children in bilingual education did not take the test: 3,000 children in the bilingual program "were not counted because they did not read English well enough in fifth grade to be tested on the English Language Stanford 9." This observation led some observers to conclude that those excluded from the test were very low in English. Ron Unz, in a letter sent to the *New York Times* (posted on his website, www.onenation.org), concluded that ". . . the review actually revealed that among all Los Angeles students who had started in a kindergarten bilingual program, less than 40 percent had learned enough English by the fifth grade even to be tested in that language." Similar sentiments were voiced in letters to the editor published by the *Times*. B. Rendahl, for example, made this accusation: "To make bilingual education look good, the L.A. schools' study had to eliminate 42 percent of the kids. These students had studied in the bilingual program for all five years of grade school and couldn't read enough English to take the test. They used 100 percent of those in the English Language Development program, however" (7 March, 1998).

Here are the facts: According to LAUSD district policy, students in bilingual education are tested in English only if they are receiving Mainstream English. Placement in Mainstream English is the last stage of a long process. It means that the students' English is considered good enough to be in an English class with native speakers of English. Of those who did not meet this criteria, and who therefore were not tested in English, *only 4 percent were still in Spanish language arts;* 96 percent were doing language arts in English, but not in the mainstream, and were doing all of their other subjects in English. All were tested on a Spanish-language version of the Stanford 9. We do not know how they would have scored on the Stanford if they had taken it in English, but we do know that they knew a considerable amount of English. On the other hand, all (97 percent) limited English proficient children not in bilingual education took the Stanford 9 in English, because it is district policy that they do so.

We do not know what would have happened if all children in bilingual education had been tested in English. It is not correct, however, to conclude that they did not know enough English to take the test. It is also not correct to assume that they were not making progress and were not being measured.

Conclusion

The cases reviewed here have several factors in common: They all have been reported as "failures" of bilingual education; all, except the last one, have been reported as success stories for alternative approaches; and they all have contributed to the assumption that bilingual education has been a disaster. Unfortunately, the evidence necessary to inform the public and the profession about what is really going on is difficult to obtain: The detailed data on the individual programs discussed here was not in professional journals and little of it is available on the web. What the public does hear and read are very brief statements in the media. Bilingual education has been condemned without a proper trial.

Postscript: The 6 Percent Argument

The most bizarre argument used by the "English for the Children" campaign in California was the claim that bilingual education had failed because ". . . each year only about 5 percent of school children [in California] classified as not proficient in English are found to have gained proficiency in English—the current system of language education has an annual failure rate of 95 percent" (English for the Children brochure).

The figure referred to is the percentage of limited English proficient children who are *reclassified* as English proficient each year. (The precise percentage is 6.2 percent in 1996, up from 5.7 percent in 1995.) To be reclassified means to reach a high enough level of English literacy to be considered fully English proficient. Calling this a "failure rate" is inaccurate and misleading. As Jeff McQuillan has pointed out to me, using this definition, a four-year college would have a 75 percent failure rate, even if all students graduated in four years.

The 6 percent figure does *not* represent the success of bilingual education. The figure is based on *all* limited English proficient children in California, not just those in bilingual education. The real issue is whether children in full bilingual programs, about 30 percent of those classified as LEP, have a lower reclassification rate. It also needs to be pointed out that reclassification is not easy to do: Some districts require that children place in the upper two-thirds of tests of English reading, which by definition one-third of the native speakers fail to accomplish.

References

Anderson, N. 1997. "Testing the Limits of Bilingual Education." *Los Angeles Times*, 8 August, A1, A16, A18.

Clark, K. 1998. *Preliminary Evaluation Report: Orange Unified School District Alternative Education Plan for LEP Students.* Stockton, CA: Clark Consulting Group.

Clegg, R. 1998. "Bilingual Litigation in California." *Wall Street Journal*, 8 June.

Cummins, J. 1981. "The Role of Primary Language Development in Promoting Educational Success for Language Minority Students." In *Schooling and Language Minority Students*, edited by the State of California Department of Bilingual Education. Los Angeles: California State University.

Elias, T. 1997. "Booting Bilingual Education." *Long Island Newsday*, 28 November.

Evergreen Unified School District. 1997. *Evaluation Study of the Former ELL Students in Seven Language Groups.* San Jose, CA: Evergreen Unified School District.

Greene, J. 1998. *A Meta-Analysis of the Effectiveness of Bilingual Education.* Claremont, CA: Tomas Rivera Policy Institute.

Jacobs, J. 1998. "If Schools Flout Prop. 227, There Will Be a Backlash." *San Jose Mercury Times*, 4 June.

Krashen, S. 1993. *The Power of Reading.* Englewood, CO: Libraries Unlimited.

———. 1996. *Under Attack: The Case Against Bilingual Education.* Culver City, CA: Language Education Associates.

Krashen, S., and D. Biber. 1988. *On Course: Bilingual Education's Success in California.* Los Angeles: California Association for Bilingual Education.

Krashen, S., and T. Terrell. 1983. *The Natural Approach: Language Acquisition in the Classroom.* New York: Prentice-Hall.

McQuillan, J. 1998. *The Literacy Crisis: False Claims and Real Solutions.* Portsmouth, NH: Heinemann.

Mitchell, D., T. Destino, and R. Karan, 1997. *Evaluation of English Language Development Programs in the Santa Ana Unified School District.* Riverside, CA: California Educational Research Cooperative, University of California, Riverside.

Nguyen, T. 1997. "Study Shows Gains from Classes Based in English." *Los Angeles Times*, Orange County edition, 2 October.

Rossell, C. 1998. Statement in the *Harvard Education Letter,* May/June.

Rossell, C., and K. Baker. 1996. "The Educational Effectiveness of Bilingual Education." *Research in the Teaching of English* 30 (1): 7–74.

Smith, C., R. Constantino, and S. Krashen. 1997. "Differences in Print Environment for Children in Beverly Hills, Compton, and Watts." *Emergency Librarian* 24 (4): 8–9.

State of California. 1997. Demographics. Available @ www.cde.ca.gov/demographics.htm.

Westminster School District. 1997. *Alternative Instruction Plan for Limited English Proficient Students, October, 1997.* Westminster, CA: Westminster School District.

Willig, A. 1985. "A Meta-Analysis of Selected Studies on the Effectiveness of Bilingual Education." *Review of Educational Research* 55 (3): 269–317.

Wright, L. 1998. "Report Finds Benefits in English Immersion." *Los Angeles Times*, Orange County edition, 18 April.

5

Bogus Argument #5

Public Opinion is Against Bilingual Education

In the recent past, two surveys of public opinion on bilingual education have been published with contradictory conclusions. Krashen (1996) claimed that respondents generally approved of bilingual education and agreed with the principles underlying it, while Rossell and Baker (1996) argue that the results of polls overestimate support for bilingual education. Interestingly, there was no overlap in the studies covered by the two surveys.

This chapter reviews all available studies discussed in Rossell and Baker as well as several studies that both surveys missed; the 1983 Houston Metropolitan Survey (Center for Public Policy), the Harris Poll (1993), de la Garza et al. (1992), Krus and Brazelton (1983), and a recent report from the Center for Equal Opportunity (1996).

The first section of this chapter reviews polls taken of the general public, the main focus of Rossell and Baker's survey. Rossell and Baker have questioned the validity of these polls. The next section responds to their arguments. We then review studies of teachers and parents as well as Rossell and Baker's comments on these polls.

Opinion Polls of the General Public

Krashen's survey, even though it was titled "Is the Public Against Bilingual Education?" focused on surveys of parents and teachers. The only exception was Hosch (1984), in which there was clear support for bilingual education. While Hosch's sample consisted of "40 individuals with a wide variety of backgrounds" (19), nearly 25 percent of the sample had children who were in or had been in bilingual programs, and nearly 40 percent were Mexican American or Mexican.

Table 5–1 presents the results of polls that attempted to get a representative sample, in which respondents were asked, in slightly different ways, whether they supported bilingual education.

It is important to examine each study in detail. For each study, we list the questions asked, as well as information about the sample.

Table 5–1
Support for Bilingual Education

	FAVORABLE (%)	UNFAVORABLE (%)	DON'T KNOW (%)
Krus and Brazelton (1983)	61		
Gallup Poll No. 20 (1988)	42	49	9
Media General/AP (1985)	36	46	18
Hakuta (1984)	70	30	
Houston Survey (1983)	68	29	3
Huddy and Sears (1990)	67		
Gallup Poll No. 23 (1991)	54		

Krus and Brazelton: In this study, "Students enrolled in an advanced class on theory of psychological measurement administered the questionnaire to their friends and members of their immediate families" (1983, 249). Forty-two subjects were interviewed.

The question represented in Table 5–1 was "Bilingual education (a) ultimately helps, (b) ultimately harms Hispanic children." In addition, the following statements were also presented to subjects:

1. "Bilingual education provides minority children with transferable skills which will allow them to be integrated into the dominant society." Fifty-seven percent of the sample agreed with this statement.

2. "Paying for bilingual education with taxpayers' money is wrong." Sixty-six percent of the respondents disagreed with this statement.

3. "Placement of Hispanic children in an educational program in which they are taught in the Spanish language will prevent them from going beyond the twelfth grade, as they will not have the English skills necessary for college." Twenty-eight percent of the respondents agreed with this statement.

(See also Krus and Stanley for a comparison of this sample with a group of "persons identified as directly involved with the Bilingual and Multicultural educational program at Arizona State University" [1985, 694]. For this pro-bilingual education sample, 100 percent supported bilingual education. For the additional questions discussed above, 78 percent agreed that bilingual education provides transferable skills, none felt that using taxpayers' money for bilingual education was wrong, and 20 percent felt that education through Spanish would prevent students from going beyond grade 12.)

Gallup 20: The question was "Would you favor or oppose the local public schools' providing instruction in a student's native language, whatever it is, in order to help him or her become a more successful learner?" The sample ($N = 2,118$) was "designed to produce an approximation of the adult civilian population, age 18 and older, living in the U.S. . . ." (1988, 45).

Media General (1985) asked "Do you think non-English-speaking students should be taught basic subjects in their own language while they learn English, or should they be placed in all-English-speaking classes?" Their sample was "a representative sample of 1,462 adults across the nation living in telephone households" including listed and nonlisted numbers. "The data projects to an estimated 161 million adults in telephone house-holds" (information provided by Stephen Shaw, Director of Research, Media General).

Note that respondents in the Media General survey were asked to comment on a version of bilingual education which could be interpreted as teaching *all* subjects in the primary language until English is acquired. As discussed below, this may not be the best version of bilingual education.

Hakuta (1984) asked "Do you think that bilingual education program is the best way for a Spanish-speaking child to learn English?" Additional details about this study are provided below.

The Houston Survey (1983) interviewed 1,000 randomly selected residents in the Houston area. It could be argued that this survey overestimated support for bilingual education; respondents were asked whether bilingual education should be available in the public schools. A "no" response could indicate that the respondent felt that bilingual education should be illegal, an extreme position.

In Huddy and Sears (1990) subjects were asked "How do you feel about bilingual education?" The sample consisted of 1,170 "Anglos," and was supplemented by 100 "non-Hispanic households" in areas of the country underrepresented in the first sample ($N = 400$). On a scale of -10 to $+10$, respondents' mean support for bilingual education was +2.29.

Gallup 23 asked 1,500 adults:

Bilingual education programs teach children who do not speak English basic subjects such as math and science in their native language, while also teaching them to speak English. Some people feel these bilingual programs should only be used until the child learns English. Others feel bilingual education should continue to be used in order to maintain the native language of children. Which opinion comes closer to your view?

The results were as follows: Until child learns English = 54 percent. Maintain native language = 37 percent.[1]

In two other polls, subjects were given a choice of different options, with bilingual education as one of the options. This kind of poll can underestimate support for bilingual education; this was clearly the case in one such poll, the 1993 Gallup Poll (No. 25).

	NATIONAL (%)	PUBLIC SCHOOL PARENTS[a] (%)
Require children to learn English in special classes at their parents' expense before they are enrolled in the public schools	25	23
Provide public school instruction in all subjects in the students' native languages while they learn English	27	30
Require students to learn English in public schools before they receive instruction in other subjects	46	45
Don't know	2	2

[a] 33 percent of sample were public-school parents.

Source: Gallup 25

In Gallup 25, only 27 percent of those interviewed (total $N =$ 1,306) appeared to support bilingual education, but subjects were asked to choose among three alternatives. Note that the option dealing with bilingual education asks whether <u>all</u> subjects should be taught in the students' primary language: "Many families who come from other countries have school-age children who cannot speak English. Which one of the following three approaches do you think is the best way for the public schools to deal with non-English-speaking students?" The table on page 70 represents the responses.

The *Time* Magazine Poll (1995) does not give a clear picture: "Which of these statements is closest to your views on bilingual education?" See table below.

The first option could be chosen by advocates of bilingual education if it does not exclude the use of other languages. But if one chooses option one, one cannot choose the others. It is not clear whether those who reject option two think that transitional bilingual education is too little or too much. Finally, those who rejected option two or three might have felt that they entailed teaching the entire curriculum in the first language.

	9/93 (%)	9/95 (%)
Public schools should teach all children in English	40	48
Public schools should teach children in their native tongue only until they know enough English to join regular classes	48	39
Public schools should teach children in their native language as long as it helps the children learn or improves their self-esteem	11	10

Source: Telephone survey "of 1,000 adult Americans," p. 49, *Time* Magazine, Oct. 6, 1995

Cain and Kiewiet (1987) was not covered in either survey. They provide data from an opinion poll conducted by telephone in California, showing that public opinion in general is not strongly anti–bilingual education. In this case, bilingual education was defined as "teaching English-speaking students in their own language as well as English" (1987, 58):

	N	FAVOR (%)	OPPOSE (%)	NO OPINION (%)
White	409	42	51	7
Black	335	63	25	12
Latino	593	69	22	9
Asian	305	51	40	9

Source: Cain and Kiewiet (1987)

Questioning the Validity of Polls

Rossell and Baker (1996) note that respondents in many polls support bilingual education, but question the validity of these results for two reasons. I refer to these arguments as the Ignorance Argument and the Trade-Off Argument.

The Ignorance Argument

Rossell and Baker argue that many respondents do not understand what bilingual education is. They note, for example, that in Huddy and Sears (1990), "only 22 percent ... of 1,170 non-Hispanic adults were able to give a roughly accurate description of bilingual education. Almost 40 percent described it as bilingualism or foreign language instruction, and 29 percent were unable to give any description at all. Despite the fact that three-quarters of respondents could not accurately describe bilingual education, a majority supported bilingual education" (171).

Huddy and Sears' classifications along with the percentage who supplied each definition from the sample of 1,170 is presented below:

PERCENTAGE SUPPLYING DEFINITION OF BILINGUAL EDUCATION	
"accurate"	
teaching foreign students in their own language	6
teaching in two languages	16
teaching English to foreign students	9
"inaccurate"	
bilingualism	18
foreign language instruction	21
no description	29

Even if we accept Huddy and Sears' classification (it can be argued that "teaching English to foreign students" is too vague to categorize as accurate or inaccurate), what is crucial is that nearly all groups of subjects were mildly positive about bilingual education. The only negative subgroup was the one that defined bilingual education as "teaching foreign students in their own language," which was very close to neutral, and consisted of a small subgroup of the sample:

SUPPORT FOR BILINGUAL EDUCATION
"Accurate" descriptions

Teaching foreign students in their own language	−.74[a]
Teaching in two languages	2.27
Teaching English to foreign students	1.75
"Inaccurate"	
Bilingualism	3.89
Foreign language instruction	2.23
No description	2.79

0 = no opinion, range from −10.25 to + 10.25
[a]small subsample

Rossell and Baker also find results of the Media General Poll to be problematic:

VIEWS ON BILINGUAL EDUCATION

	yes	no	don't know
Successful in teaching basic subjects	38%	23%	39%
Successful in teaching English	42%	24%	34%
Support for bilingual education	36%	46%	18%

They note that about 40 percent said they didn't know if bilingual education was successful, but only 18 percent "lacked an opinion on whether non-English-speaking students should learn in their native language in school. In other words, it appears that some of the respondents who had no opinion on the efficacy of bilingual education were nevertheless willing to express a preference" (1996, 166).

There is a simple explanation: Those who did not know whether bilingual education was successful or not probably did not support it, nor did those who felt it was not successful; those who felt it was successful did support it. In other words, those who were in the "don't know" column for the first two questions probably migrated to the "no" column for the third question. If this is true, results of this poll underestimate potential support for bilingual education; with more knowledge, more might have supported it.

In support of this analysis, note the close correspondence in the "yes" column among the three questions; the percentage who felt that bilingual education was successful in teaching basic subjects was not significantly different from the percentage that supported bilingual education, while the difference between the percentage who felt bilingual education was successful in teaching English was just barely significantly larger than the percentage supporting bilingual education:

COMPARISON	DIFFERENCE (%)	SAMPLING TOLERANCE[a] (%)
Successful in teaching basic subjects vs. support for bil. ed.	2	6
Successful in teaching English vs. support for bil. ed.	6	6

[a]Sampling tolerances supplied by Media General.

The Trade-Off Argument

Rossell and Baker also argue that polls overestimate the support for bilingual education because they do not always ask "the trade-off question": They do not ask whether the respondent would support bilingual education if it meant fewer resources or less time devoted to other things, maintaining that "more of something usually means less of something else" (163).

Rossell and Baker support this point by noting that in several studies respondents appear to agree that the aim of bilingual education should be to encourage students to enter English-only classes as soon as possible, but also agree that programs should aim to maintain the Spanish language and culture. As an example of this, Rossell and Baker discuss Hakuta (1984):

> In Hakuta's 1984 survey of 216 adults in New Haven (37 of them Spanish-speaking), 76 percent of the respondents agreed that the emphasis of bilingual education should be to encourage students to enter English-only classes as soon as possible, yet 58 percent agreed that the emphasis should be on maintaining the Spanish language and culture of the children . . . it is clear that unless respondents are explicitly asked to consider the trade-off, they will not. In this case they should have been asked whether they wanted to emphasize maintaining the Spanish language even if it meant that a student's entry into an English-only classroom would not occur quickly. (171)

Rossell and Baker assume that these goals are contradictory, that more time devoted to Spanish will necessarily mean less progress in developing academic English.

The point of bilingual education, however, is that more education in the first language, when done correctly, can mean faster development of English literacy: When students learn to read in their primary language, it is much easier to learn to read in English, and because the first language will be more comprehensible, it is easier to learn to read in the first language. In addition, background knowledge gained through the first language can greatly enhance comprehension of material presented in the second language. There is no trade-off. Respondents who want both English and Spanish literacy are not contradicting themselves.[2]

An Additional Teacher Study: The 1993 Harris Poll

The Harris Poll was a national survey of teachers, 97 percent of whom were not Hispanic. Responses to a question dealing with bilingual education appear to be nonsupportive:

> Do you think government policy should promote bilingual education programs that teach English and teach other substantive subjects in a child's native language, or should policy mandate that substantive subjects be taught in English?
>
> Government should promote teaching substantive subjects in native language = 34%.
>
> Substantive subjects should be taught in English = 64%.
>
> Not sure = 2%.

Note that respondents could be rejecting a version of bilingual education in which all subjects are taught in the first language, with nothing ever taught in English. In one plan, the gradual-exit plan (Krashen 1996), subject matter is taught in the primary language only until the child knows enough English to follow instruction in English. "Transition" occurs gradually, a few subjects at a time, as they become comprehensible. The plan also includes sheltered subject matter teaching in English as a transition between all primary language and the mainstream. It is quite possible that many of those who felt that "substantive subjects should be taught in English" would have agreed with this kind of approach.

Additional Studies of Parents

The de la Garza et al. (1992) study was not covered either by Rossell and Baker or by Krashen. De la Garza et al. surveyed adults whose national origins were Mexican, Puerto Rican, and Cuban. The items discussed here were answered by a subgroup of the sample, citizens of the United States (Mexican origin, $N = 878$; Puerto Rican = 587; Cuban = 312). Attitudes toward bilingual education were very positive:

ATTITUDE TOWARD BILINGUAL EDUCATION	MEXICAN (%)	PUERTO RICAN (%)	CUBAN (%)
Strongly support or support	80	87	88
Uncertain	13	7	19
Oppose or strongly oppose	7	6	3
Percentage willing to pay more taxes for bilingual education	69	70	54

Responses to the next question accurately reflect what bilingual education is about: Respondents understood that its goal is bilingualism.

OBJECTIVE OF BILINGUAL EDUCATION	MEXICAN (%)	PUERTO RICAN (%)	CUBAN (%)
To learn English	15	12	10
To learn two languages	70	74	77
To maintain Spanish language and culture	9	8	5
Other	6	7	7.5

It is also clear that this group is pro-English:

U.S. CITIZENS AND RESIDENTS SHOULD LEARN ENGLISH	MEXICAN	PUERTO RICAN	CUBAN
Strongly agree or agree	91	93	93

Lambert and Taylor's (1990) study of public-school parents in the Detroit area, also not covered in either survey, showed support for a nonextreme version of bilingual education among most groups, except for white working-class and white middle-class parents.

ON A SCALE OF 1 TO 7, SHOULD THE HOME LANGUAGE BE USED "FOR PART OF THE TEACHING AND LEARNING IN PUBLIC SCHOOLS"? (NO = 1, NEUTRAL = 4, YES = 7)	
Group	Support level
Polish American	4.52
Arab American	6.74
Albanian American	6.21
Mexican American	5.55
Puerto-Rican American	6.63
White working class	2.42
White middle class	3.22
Black Hamtrack	4.59
Black Pontiac	3.86

Are Parents Confused?
A Discussion of the ETS Study

The Educational Testing Service (ETS) survey (Baratz-Snowden et al. 1988) of parents of language-minority students shows wide support for bilingual education. Rossell and Baker, however, claim that the report contains "fascinating inconsistencies in parental support for various options" (1996, 172), and these inconsistencies suggest that respondents were confused about bilingual education.

Parents were asked whether they thought bilingual, transitional, or immersion programs were a good idea. As Rossell and Baker note, all three programs were supported, which prompted Rossell and Baker to conclude that "regardless of the type (of program), . . . an overwhelming majority of parents think language-minority children should get some kind of help, particularly in learning English, and they are not clear about differences between types of help" (177). It is important to point out, however, that parents were not asked to choose between these programs: one-third of the sample was asked about maintenance bilingual education, one-third about transitional, and one-third about immersion. Agreeing that a certain program would be a good idea for helping students who don't speak English might simply mean that respondents thought that doing the program would be better than doing nothing (submersion). Supporters of bilingual education would probably respond positively to all three options, when compared to submersion (sink or swim).

Rossell and Baker claim that "most of these parents do not think native language proficiency should be taught in school" (174). They base this statement partly on responses to the following question: (If a child does not speak or understand English very well) would it help the child if classes were taught using the non-English language? Twenty-nine percent of the respondents categorizing themselves as Mexican Americans responded positively, as did 28 percent of the Asian respondents.

Rossell and Baker note that this question was not actually asked in this way, but is a result of their reanalysis of the data in the survey. After reviewing Baratz-Snowden et al. in some detail, I was unable to discover how Rossell and Baker arrived at these figures.

In addition, Rossell and Baker claim that "almost half

of Mexican American and 60 percent of Asian parents think that teaching in the native tongue interferes with English." The full table of results, from Table 19 of the survey, is presented below:

DO YOU THINK TEACHING IN A NON-ENGLISH LANGUAGE INTERFERES WITH LEARNING ENGLISH?

	N	yes	no	don't know
Asian	865	60	33	8
Mexican American	901	43	51	6
Puerto Rican (N)[a]	288	33	62	6
Puerto Rican (S)[b]	340	54	44	2
Cuban	501	19	79	2

[a]N = NAEP sample
[b]S = supplementary sample

Source: Baratz-Snowden et al. 1988, Table 19

Clearly, quite a few parents do not think that teaching in the primary language interferes with acquiring English (80 percent of the Cuban parents and 62 percent of one of the Puerto Rican samples.) Nevertheless, quite a few do; it is possible that this question was interpreted as referring to programs in which all teaching is in the primary language.

Baratz-Snowden et al. also asked parents "In what language should non-English students be taught?" for reading and writing and for basic subjects. Their results, expressed in percentages, are presented on page 82.

	ONLY IN ENGLISH (%)	IN BOTH ENGLISH & NON-ENGLISH (%)	ONLY IN NON-ENGLISH (%)
Read and Write			
Asian	67	32	.1
Mexican American	28	70	0
Puerto Rican (N)[a]	21	77	.8
Puerto Rican (S)[b]	16	82	1
Cuban	20	80	0
Basic Subjects			
Asian	68	30	.1
Mexican American	39	56	0
Puerto Rican (N)[a]	29	70	1.1
Puerto Rican (S)[b]	27	70	1.4
Cuban	50	48	.8

[a]N= NAEP sample
[b]S = supplementary sample

All percentages rounded off except for the last column.

Source: Baratz-Snowden et al. 1988, Table 24

This table shows clear support for bilingual education, especially when used for developing literacy. Rossell and Baker argue that it is another indication of confusion: Because 70 percent of Mexican American parents preferred that reading and writing be taught in both languages, and 43 percent thought that teaching in the non-English language interferes with learning English (see above), then 27 percent of them must be confused. There is, however, an easy explanation: As noted earlier, some parents might have interpreted the question about teaching in the first language interfering with English as meaning teaching *exclusively* in the first language, an option that very few people support.

Rossell and Baker's next "confusion argument" is based on responses to this question: "Do you think the schools should teach non-English-language-speaking children the non-English language if it means less time for teaching them (English, Math, Science, Art, Music)?" Parents responded negatively to all of these options. Many supporters of bilingual education would probably also respond negatively to this question, as discussed earlier. The point is that good bilingual programs do not force students to sacrifice in this way. Unfortunately, the wording of the question presupposes that instruction in the primary language inevitably means less time for other things, and suggests less English language development.

Rossell and Baker's final "confusion argument" is based on responses to an open question in which parents were asked the three most important things they wanted children to learn from school. The most popular answers were mastery of academic subjects, English language competence, and "general education," while "learn about child's ethnic heritage" and "learn both languages" were not mentioned often. They conclude from these results that "there is, for all practical purposes, no desire on the part of . . . parents for the schools to teach ethnic heritage" (181). The survey results are, however, reasonable. The point is that the proper use of the primary language in bilingual education programs leads to the attainment of the goals of mastery of academic subjects and English language competence. Note also that the low rank of "ethnic heritage" and "learn both languages" does not reflect lack of concern with these goals: Subjects were asked the *three* most important things the parents wanted their children to learn—it is unlikely that heritage culture and heritage language development would be in the top three.

Center for Equal Opportunity

The Center for Equal Opportunity (CEO) survey included 600 randomly selected Hispanic parents with children currently in school. About 80 percent of the sample said that their children were not in "a program in school for children who need help with English" (1996, 10) and the same percentage said their children were never asked to be in such a program. The programs the children participated in were hardly industrial-strength first-language programs: Parents reported that about 10 percent had no Spanish at all, 23 percent were only a "small part" in Spanish, 29 percent were half in Spanish, and 27 percent were "mostly in Spanish." Of the entire sample of 600 parents, ninety-three had children who were in or who had been in a special program, and of those ninety-three, only twenty-five of them were in programs conducted mostly in Spanish, or 4 percent of the total. This is contrary to the view of some critics, who claim that Hispanic children throughout the United States are taught in Spanish-only programs.

Of those whose children had been in such a program 74.5 percent reported that their children were in the program three years or less. While this latter figure underestimates the length of time a typical child participates, because it includes children still in the program, it suggests that children do not stay in special programs very long, also contrary to the claims of critics.

Not surprisingly, parents were pro-English: 51 percent rated "learning to read, write, and speak English" as the most important thing children might learn in school and 19 percent rated it second. Many supporters of bilingual education would, of course, also rate this goal very highly.

The controversial questions were these:

(1) In your opinion, should children of Hispanic background living in the United States be taught to read and write Spanish

before they are taught English, or should they be taught English as soon as possible?

The results:

English as soon as possible = 63%

Spanish before English = 17%

Same time = 17%

This is a difficult question to answer. One would expect parents to respond that children should be taught English as soon as possible. Bilingual education, it has been argued, is the best way to make this happen. The way the question is phrased, however, suggests that learning to read and write in Spanish will not help children to learn to read and write English "as soon as possible."

Shin asked a similar question, but did so more precisely, asking whether respondees felt that "developing literacy through the first language facilitates literacy development in English." The language-minority parents she questioned supported this position:

Hispanic parents = 53% (Shin and Gribbons 1996)

Korean parents = 88% (Shin and Kim 1996)

Hmong parents = 52% (Shin and Lee 1996)

Shin's question does not presuppose that learning to read in the first language slows down the acquisition of English literacy; the CEO's version does.

(2) In general, which of the following comes closest to your opinion?

1. My child should be taught his/her academic courses in Spanish, even if it means he/she will spend less time learning English.

2. My child should be taught his/her academic courses in English, because he/she will spend more time learning English.

The results:

Spanish = 12%

English = 81%

As noted previously, such questions are flawed: First, they give the impression that in option one, all courses will be taught in Spanish with nothing in English. Second, they suggest that learning content through Spanish will not help English language development. It is thus no surprise that respondees vote for English.

Shin also attempted to ask this question more precisely, asking whether parents agreed that "Learning subject matter through the first language helps make subject matter study in English more comprehensible." Support was not as strong as it was for the question on literacy, but Shin found more support for first-language content teaching than the CEO did:

Hispanic parents = 34% (33% were "not sure") (Shin and Gribbons 1996)

Korean parents = 47% (Shin and Kim 1996)

Hmong parents = 60% (Shin and Lee 1996)

Summary and Conclusions

The results of the polls discussed here are summarized in Table 5–2. Responses are clearly more negative when statements and questions can easily be interpreted as supporting an extreme version of bilingual education in which only the primary language is used (Harris Poll 1993, Baratz-Snowden et al. 1998; *Time* 1995; CEO 1996) or one in which all subject matter is taught in the primary language until English is acquired (Media General 1985; Gallup Poll No. 25 1993).

When subjects are asked about using both languages

Table 5–2
Summary of Polls on Bilingual Education

SUPPORTIVE	TYPE OF QUESTION
Krus and Brazelton	Global (BE "helps" or "harms")
Hakuta	Global (BE "is the best way . . . to learn English")
Houston	Global (should BE be "available")
Huddy and Sears	Global
de la Garza et al.	Global
Lambert and Taylor	"Part of the day"[a]
Baratz-Snowden et al.	Teach literacy, subjects in both languages
Gallup 23	Teach "basic subjects . . . in . . . native language"
Cain and Kieweit	Teach in own language "as well as English"[a]

[a]all groups supportive except whites

NOT SUPPORTIVE	TYPE OF QUESTION
Gallup 20	Teach "basic subjects in primary language"
Gallup 25	"Provide instruction in all subjects . . . in . . . native language"
Media General	"Should be taught basic subjects in their own language"
Time Magazine	"Should teach . . . in native language until they know enough English"

continues

Table 5–2
continued

Harris	"Teach substantive subjects . . . in . . . native language"
Baratz-Snowden et al.	"Teaching in non-English language interferes with English"
CEO	"Teach academic courses in Spanish, even if it means . . . less time learning English"
	Teach reading and writing in Spanish before they are taught English, "or should they be taught English as soon as possible?"

(Baratz-Snowden et al. 1998) or are asked about bilingual education globally, they are much more positive (Krus and Brazelton 1983, Hakuta 1984, Huddy and Sears 1990, Houston Survey 1983, de la Garza et al. 1992). Baratz-Snowden et al. provide evidence that this generalization is correct: When it is made clear that both English and the primary language are to be included, subjects are supportive of bilingual education; when this is not clear, they react differently. This is a more plausible explanation than Rossell and Baker's, who maintain only that respondees were confused. The only exceptions to this generalization is Gallup No. 23, which was supportive despite the vagueness of the question.

These results converge with those of Krashen (1996), who reviewed studies of parents, teachers, and school administrators, and found consistent support for bilingual education when the question was asked globally. Polls that appear to present counterevidence typically present a view of bilingual education that few of its supporters would endorse.[3]

Notes

1. I use Rossell and Baker's citation for this study as well as their description. I was unable to find it in the 1991 or 1992 Gallup Poll results as published in the *Phi Delta Kappan*.

2. Rossell and Baker's characterization of Hakuta's study is slightly inaccurate and incomplete. The total number of subjects surveyed was 216, but they were divided into two groups, a general sample and a Spanish-speaking sample. The data summarized by Rossell and Baker was from the general sample only. In addition, both groups were very positive about bilingual education, which was not mentioned by Rossell and Baker. Here is some detail from the study:

	GENERAL (%) AGREE	SPANISH-SPEAKING (%) AGREE
Do you think the emphasis should be to encourage students to enter English-only classes as quickly as possible?	76	89
Do you think the emphasis should be to maintain the Spanish language and culture of the children?	58	82
Do you think that bilingual education program is the best way for a Spanish-speaking child to learn English?	70	74
In your opinion, should the amount of funding for bilingual education classes be increased, decreased, or kept the same?		
decrease	18	6
kept the same	32	17
increase	50	78

Source: Hakuta (1984)

3. Some of the opposition to bilingual education is not, it appears, based on whether it is good pedagogy. As Huddy and Sears noted, "There was considerable anti-Hispanic sentiment with the sample" (1990, 128), and reported, not surprisingly, that indicators of this kind of attitude were predictive of objection to bilingual education, as shown by the multiple regression analysis presented below:

SIGNIFICANT PREDICTORS OF OPPOSITION TO BILINGUAL EDUCATION	BETA
Symbolic racism: attitudes toward demands for special treatment	.23
Nationalism: anti-immigrant attitudes	.06
Inegalitarian values	.05
Conservative political ideology	.06
In favor of cutting spending for foreign language instruction	.27
$r^2 = .259$	

Source: Huddy and Sears (1990)

In addition, in the Media General report, 45 percent of those who classified themselves as "liberal" supported bilingual education, while only 33 percent of those who classified themselves as "conservative" did so (36 percent of those who were neither liberal nor conservative supported bilingual education).

It must be emphasized that anti-Hispanic sentiment and political orientation did *not* explain a large percentage of the respondents' attitudes toward bilingual education (note that $r^2 = .259$ for all predictors combined in Huddy and Sears' study).

References

Baratz-Snowden, J., D. Rock, J. Pollack, and G. Wilder. 1988. *Parent Preference Study*. Princeton, NJ: Educational Testing Service.

Cain, B., and D. Kiewiet. 1987. "Latinos and the 1984 Election: A Comparative Perspective." In *Ignored Voices: Public Opinion Polls and the Latino Community*, edited by R. de la Garza. Austin, TX: The Center for Mexican American Studies, University of Texas at Austin.

Center for Equal Opportunity. 1996. *The Importance of Learning English*. Washington, DC: Center for Equal Opportunity.

Center for Public Policy. 1983. *Metropolitan Area Survey*. Center for Public Policy, 515 Hoffman Hall College of Social Science, University of Houston, Houston, TX 77004.

de la Garza, R., L. DeSipio, F. C. Garcia, J. Garcia, and A. Falcon. 1992. *Latino Voices: Mexican, Puerto Rican, and Cuban Perspectives on American Politics*. Boulder, CO: Westview Press.

Elam, S., L. Rose, and A. Gallup. 1993. "The 25th Annual Gallup Poll of the Public's Attitude Toward the Public Schools." *Phi Delta Kappan* 95: 137–152.

Gallup, A., and S. Elam. 1988. "The 20th Annual Gallup Poll of the Public's Attitudes Toward the Public Schools." *Phi Delta Kappan* 70: 33–46.

Hakuta, K. 1984. "Bilingual Education in the Public Eye: A Case Study of New Haven, Connecticut." *NABE Journal* 9: 53–76.

Harris, L. 1993. *National Survey of Teachers*. New York: Louis Harris and Associates, 630 Fifth Avenue, New York, NY 10111.

Hosch, H. 1984. *Attitudes Toward Bilingual Education: A View from the Border*. El Paso: Texas Western Press.

Huddy, L., and D. Sears. 1990. "Qualified Public Support for Bilingual Education: Some Policy Implications." *Annals of the American Academy of Political and Social Science* 508: 119–134.

Krashen, S. 1996. *Under Attack: The Case Against Bilingual Education*. Culver City, CA: Language Education Associates.

Krus, D., and J. Brazelton. 1983. "Contributions to Psychohistory: VIII. Perspectives on Bilingual Education in the Austrian Empire and the United States of America: Is the Assumption of Temporal Contenation of Linguistic and Territorial Separatism Valid?" *Psychological Reports* 53: 247–254.

Krus, D., and M. Stanley. 1985. "Validity of the Attitudes Toward Bilingual Education Scale with Respect to Group Discrimination." *Educational and Psychological Measurement* 45: 693–698.

Lambert, W., and D. Taylor. 1990. *Coping with Cultural and Racial Diversity in Urban America.* New York: Praeger.

Media General Poll. November, 1985. Media General, P.O. Box 85333, Richmond, VA 23293-0001.

Rossell, C., and K. Baker. 1996. *Bilingual Education in Massachusetts: The Emperor Has No Clothes.* Boston: The Pioneer Institute for Public Policy Research.

Shin, F., and B. Gribbons. 1996. "Hispanic Parent Perceptions and Attitudes of Bilingual Education." *The Journal of Mexican American Educators* 16–22.

Shin, F., and S. Kim. 1996. "Korean Parent Perceptions and Attitudes of Bilingual Education." In *Current Issues in Asian and Pacific American Education,* edited by R. Endo, C. Park, J. Tsuchida, and A. Abbayani. Covina, CA: Pacific Asian Press.

Shin, F., and B. Lee. 1996. "Hmong Parents: What Do They Think About Bilingual Education?" *Pacific Educational Research Journal* 8: 65–71.

Time Magazine. 1995. "Rise of English-Only." 6 October: 49.

Postscript: Public Opinion in California

During the recent Proposition 227 campaign in California, public opinion polls were consistently interpreted as showing strong support for English-only approaches and hostility to bilingual education. A closer look at the polls, however, shows that this was not the case. Contrary to popular opinion, the public was surprisingly supportive of bilingual education. Their support of Proposition 227, it appears, was based on a serious misconception, the belief that a vote for 227 was a vote in support of English.

The *L.A. Times* Poll: October 15, 1997

In the early months of the campaign, the "English for the Children" campaign literature asserted that Latino parents were opposed to bilingual education, claiming that a "recent *L.A. Times* survey of Latino residents in Orange County showed 83 percent opposition to the methods of 'bilingual education'." Here is the question asked, and the results (750 residents of Orange County participated):

Which of the following do you most prefer for teaching students who speak limited English?

	TOTAL (%)	LATINOS (%)
Mostly English with some help in their native language	59	57
Only in English as soon as they enroll in school	32	26
Native language until they are ready to learn English	7	17

Source: L.A. Times, October 15, 1997

Few supporters of bilingual education would choose the third option, which calls for no English exposure at all at the beginning. In other words, only 17 percent of the Latino respondents supported an extreme version of bilingual education. In addition, only 26 percent preferred programs with no instruction in the first language.

Option one, while not exactly what is proposed in the gradual exit bilingual plan described in Krashen (1996), is the closest to it, and it received the most support, in agreement with the rest of the research on attitudes toward bilingual education.

The *L.A. Times* Poll: April 13, 1998

Despite the headline, "Bilingual Education Ban Widely Supported" (*L.A. Times*, April 13, 1998), this poll of 1,409 adults also showed very strong support for the use of the primary language in school. The poll included this question, which I present along with the percentage who agreed with each statement: "Which of these statements comes closest to your point of view?"

> Students should be taught only in English because that is the best way for them to learn English = 32%.
>
> Students should be assisted in their native language for only a brief period of time, such as a year or two = 39%.
>
> Students should be taught in both their native language and English as long as educators and parents believe it is necessary = 25%.
>
> Don't know = 4%.

Thus, 64 percent of those responding supported some form of bilingual education, with only 32 percent supporting English-only. This result is practically identical to that of the 15 October poll, in which 66 percent supported at least some use of the first language and, once again, 32 percent preferred English-only.

Why, then, did respondees also show strong support for Proposition 227, a measure that virtually eliminates bilingual education and that substitutes something very close to English-only? On its website, the *L.A. Times* revealed the answer: When those who said they would vote for 227 were asked why, 63 percent said it was because of the importance of English; only 9 percent said it was because they felt that bilingual education was not effective, and only 6 percent said it was because they preferred immersion. This suggests that support for 227 was to a large extent because people felt they were voting "for English."

The USC Study

Our suspicions were confirmed in our USC (University of Southern California) study. Jim Crawford noted that the following kind of question is typically asked of voters in polls:

> There is an initiative on the June primary ballot that would require all public school instruction to be conducted in English and for students not fluent in English to be placed in a short-term English immersion program. If the June primary were being held today, would you vote for or against this measure?

This kind of question can be easily interpreted as "Are you in favor of children getting intensive English instruction?" and does not reflect what is in Proposition 227. A more accurate question, Crawford suggested, would be one like this one:

> There is an initiative on the June primary ballot that would severely restrict the use of the child's native language in school. This initiative would limit special help in English to one year (180 school days). After this time, limited English proficient children would be expected to know enough English to do school work at the same level as native speakers of English their age. The initiative would dismantle many current programs that have been demonstrated to be successful in helping children acquire English, and would hold teachers financially responsible if

they violate this policy. If passed, schools would have 60 days to conform to the new policy. If the June primary were being held today, would you vote for or against this measure?

Students in my language education class asked 251 voters either the original question 1 or the modified question 2 and the data was analyzed by Haeyoung Kim. The difference between the responses to the two questions was huge (and statistically significant): While 57 percent supported the original version, only 15 percent supported the modified version, a result that confirmed our suspicions that few people knew what was in Proposition 227, and when they found out, they did not support it. (Unfortunately, despite numerous attempts, we were unable to get this information to many voters.)

$N = 251$	FOR	DON'T KNOW	AGAINST
original	4 (57%)	7 (13%)	9 (30%)
modified	18 (15%)	17 (14%)	86 (71%)

chi square = 51.51, df = 2, p < .001

This brief survey of California polls gives results very consistent with the results of previous polls on bilingual education; there is little objection to providing children with help in their primary language in school.

6

A Note on Greene's A Meta-Analysis of the Effectiveness of Bilingual Education

reene's *Meta-analysis* is a short report that should have a profound impact on the field.[1] In 1996, Rossell and Baker published an analysis of the effectiveness of bilingual education, and concluded that there was no evidence that bilingual programs were superior to English-only options for limited English proficient children. Greene has reworked the data Rossell and Baker analyzed, applying a more rigorous and precise approach called meta-analysis, thus repeating what Willig did in 1985, when she reanalyzed the results of Baker and de Kanter (1983).

Rossell and Baker used a "vote-counting" technique in their review of studies of bilingual education. If a study showed that students in bilingual classes did better than those in nonbilingual classes, bilingual education got one "vote," and if those in nonbilingual classes did better, nonbilingual got one "vote." A problem with vote-getting is that a study can be counted as favoring one method even when it is only slightly better. Winning by a little and winning by a lot count the same. Meta-analysis takes this into consideration by assigning to each study a number that indicates the size of the effect—how big the difference was between the treatments. Greene reviewed the studies Rossell and Baker did, but calculated, for each study, the "effect size." An effect size of zero means no difference between the groups. A positive effect size meant students in bilingual education did better, a negative effect size means that students in nonbilingual groups did better.[2]

Greene's analysis differs in another way from Rossell and Baker's: He only included studies with a treatment of at least one year. He did, however, accept Rossell and Baker's other criteria for whether a study was included in the analysis (use of a control group, control for initial differences in the groups or randomization, use of standardized tests in English, use of appropriate statistical tests).[3] He found eleven studies that were eligible for analysis, computed the average effect size for English reading, math, and Spanish reading. This average effect size was positive, which meant that on the average, bilingual education had a positive effect. This replicated Willig's results in her reanalysis of Baker and de Kanter's vote-getting review. Greene reported an average effect size for English reading of .21, which statisticians consider to be modest. It was, however, statistically significantly different from zero, which meant it is unlikely that it happened by chance. (This means that the average student in the bilingual groups scored .21 standard deviations above the mean of the average student in the nonbilingual education groups. According to the Tomas Rivera Center, minority students score about one standard deviation below nonminority students; bilingual education, then, makes up about 20 percent of the gap. For math, the effect size was .12, while for Spanish reading it was .74.)[4]

Greene's analysis may have underestimated the effect of bilingual education: First, the average duration of program in the eleven studies he analyzed was only two years. Cummins and others have argued that the full impact of education in the primary language is not felt until more time has gone by (see, e.g., Thomas and Collier [1997] for extensive discussion). Second, Greene did not attempt to account for the kind of bilingual education model used; some kinds of programs are more effective than others (e.g., Legaretta 1979). Of the three published studies he included, "bilingual education" is not described in any detail in two of them (Bacon, Kidd, and Seaberg [1982] and Rossell [1990]). In one (Bacon, Kidd, and Seaberg [1982]), paraprofessionals were used and in another (Kaufman [1968]) "bilingual education" was direct instruction in reading for seventh graders who could already read in English to some extent. Current theory predicts that in well-designed programs with subject matter teaching in the first language, literacy development in the first language, and quality comprehensible input in English, the effects will be larger.

According to Pyle (1998), supporters of Proposition 227, a proposal to end bilingual education in California, have criticized Greene's study because the studies are "old" (the eleven studies are from 1968 to 1991). It must be pointed out, however, that Greene simply reanalyzed the studies Rossell and Baker considered, a review that anti–bilingual education critics have applauded. In addition, I ran a correlation between year of publication of the study and the effect size reported: the correlation was close to zero (r = .04) for the ten studies that reported an effect size for English reading, meaning that earlier studies and later studies had similar effects.

Notes

1. Greene's report is also available on Jim Crawford's website, http://ourworld.compuserve.com/homepages/jwcrawford/greene/htm. The report is also discussed in a "Policy Brief" issued by the Tomas Rivera Center, March, 1998.

2. For those who survived Statistics 1, here is how effect size is computed. You take the mean of the experimental group and subtract the mean of the comparison group and divide the whole thing by the standard deviation of the control group (or the pooled standard deviation of both groups). This "effect size" can be converted to a correlation coefficient by a simple formula. Clear introductions to the calculation of effect sizes and their use in meta-analyses are found in Wolf (1986) and Light and Pillemer (1984). (It should also be noted Greene used a technique that allowed him to take the size of the sample of the study into consideration.)

3. Greene notes that I "proposed that Rossell and Baker include additional studies favorable to bilingual education even though they do not meet the criteria" (1998, 3). This is not quite what I proposed (Krashen 1996). I only pointed out that while Rossell and Baker excluded a number of studies for not randomizing or otherwise controlling for existing differences among groups, we have no reason to suspect such differences exist, and that when a number of studies like this are done, one has a kind of randomization. The results of these studies should not be ignored. I agree, however, with Greene that meta-analyses should not include them (or should deal with them as a separate group). In addition, I pointed out that for many of the studies Rossell and Baker accepted favoring nonbilingual groups, sample sizes were very small or the duration of treatment was very short or the comparison itself was not valid (comparison of different kinds of Canadian immersion).

4. Willig's results are nearly identical to Greene's, which adds to the reliability and plausibility of his results. Willig (1985) also reported an overall effect size of .21 for English reading, adjusted for method of calculating effect size (there are several alternative methods), method of controlling for initial differences, and type of score reported (e.g., raw scores, percentiles, and so on). For mathematics, Willig reported an adjusted effect size of .18, very close to Greene's .12. For total language, when tested in the non-English language, Willig reported an adjusted effect size of .73, while Greene reported .74. Finally, Willig reported a larger effect size

when initial differences were controlled by randomization rather than by other methods, and so did Greene. The similarity is not because both researchers looked at the same studies. Only four studies were included in both analyses.

References

Bacon, H., G. Kidd, and J. Seaberg. 1982. "The Effectiveness of Bilingual Instruction with Cherokee Indian Students." *Journal of American Indian Education* (February): 34–43.

Baker, K., and A. de Kanter. 1983. "Federal Policy and the Effectiveness of Bilingual Education." In *Bilingual Education,* edited by K. Baker and A. de Kanter. Lexington, MA: DC Heath.

Greene, J. 1998. *A Meta-Analysis of the Effectiveness of Bilingual Education.* Claremont, CA: Tomas Rivera Policy Institute.

Krashen, S. 1996. *Under Attack: The Case Against Bilingual Education.* Culver City, CA: Language Education Associates.

Kaufman, M. 1968. "Will Instruction in Reading Spanish Affect Ability in Reading English?" *The Journal of Reading* 11: 521–527.

Legarreta, D. 1979. "The Effects of Program Models on Language Acquisition by Spanish-Speaking Children." *TESOL Quarterly* 13 (4): 521–534.

Light, R., and D. Pillemer. 1984. *Summing Up: The Science of Reviewing Research.* Cambridge, MA: Harvard University Press.

Pyle, A. 1998. "Opinions Vary on Studies That Back Bilingual Classes." *Los Angeles Times,* 2 March, sec. B1, B3.

Rossell, C. 1990. "The Effectiveness of Educational Alternatives for Limited English-Proficient Children." In *Learning in Two Languages,* edited by G. Imhoff. New Brunswick, NJ: Transaction.

Rossell, C., and K. Baker. 1996. "The Educational Effectiveness of Bilingual Education." *Research in the Teaching of English* 30 (1): 7–74.

Thomas, W., and V. Collier. 1997. *School Effectiveness for Language Minority Students.* Washington, DC: National Clearinghouse for Bilingual Education.

Willig, A. 1985. "A Meta-Analysis of Selected Studies on the Effectiveness of Bilingual Education." *Review of Educational Research* 55 (3): 269–317.

Wolf, F. 1986. *Meta-Analysis.* Thousand Oaks, CA: Sage Publications.

Index

103